THE ULTIMATE
NEW YORK RANGERS
TRIVIA BOOK

A Collection of Amazing Trivia Quizzes and Fun Facts for Die-Hard Rangers Fans!

Ray Walker

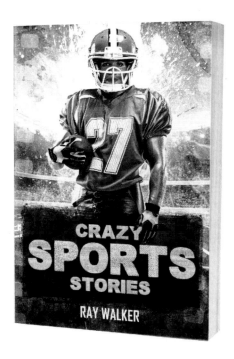

CONTENTS

INTRODUCTION

Even non-hockey fans know who the New York Rangers are, as the "Original Six" team has been delivering the goods in the Big Apple since the 1926-27 NHL season. They had some stiff local competition from the New York Americans until 1942 but persevered and were still standing when their rivals folded shop.

Rangers fans are loyal, passionate, and as vocal as any in the world when they get behind their team. The rafters usually rock at Madison Square Garden during Rangers games, especially when they're taking on one of their heated or local rivals.

The team shot out of the gate and struck gold in the matter of two years as they hoisted their first Stanley Cup in just their second season of existence. Unfortunately, they've only won three more championships since then in 10 Stanley Cup Finals, but they've never stopped entertaining their fans.

Curse or no curse, the club went over 50 years between Cup celebrations, from 1940 to 1994, but their loyal fans never deserted them. Plenty of stories are still told regarding this period as the club worked toward turning its fortunes around.

The Rangers are a fixture in New York City—the same as the

Empire State Building, Statue of Liberty, Times Square, Central Park, and Broadway. In fact, the club's original nickname was the Broadway Blueshirts.

Some of the game's greatest players have graced the ice at Madison Square Garden, such as Hall-of-Famers Frank Boucher, Harry Howell, Rod Gilbert, Phil Esposito, Brian Leetch, Mark Messier, and, of course, the great Wayne Gretzky.

This book you are holding in your hands contains a multitude of trivia, facts, and information about the beloved Rangers organization, from their roots up until the conclusion of the 2019-20 regular NHL season.

It's separated into 15 different chapters with each having a specific topic. Every section offers a total of 20 multiple-choice and true-false questions with the answers on a separate page. The chapters also come with 10 "Did You Know? " facts and stories about the organization.

This is the ideal way to freshen up on your Rangers history and to then test it out by challenging fellow fans, friends, and family members in trivia contests. It's meant to educate and entertain while bringing back memories to the team's supporters.

The Rangers may be going through another Stanley Cup drought, as they haven't hoisted the Stanley Cup since 1994, but their fans are still right behind them and letting the opposition know it during each game.

Hopefully, this trivia book will remind you why you're such a passionate Rangers fan.

CHAPTER 1:

ORIGINS & HISTORY

QUIZ TIME!

1. Who founded the Rangers franchise?

    a. Tommy Gorman
    b. Lester Patrick
    c. Tex Rickard
    d. Conn Smythe

2. When did the Rangers win their first Stanley Cup?

    a. 1932-33
    b. 1939-40
    c. 1926-27
    d. 1927-28

3. In their inaugural season, the club finished first in the American Division.

    a. True
    b. False

4. How many times has the team made the playoffs in their first 93 seasons?

a. 60

b. 53

c. 59

d. 47

5. In possibly their worst season, how many wins did the team muster in 1943-44?

    a. 11

    b. 6

    c. 5

    d. 8

6. Who coached the team to a league-high 112 points and a fourth Stanley Cup in 1993-94?

    a. Colin Campbell

    b. Mike Keenan

    c. Roger Neilson

    d. Ron Smith

7. Which year did the Rangers sign free agent Wayne Gretzky?

    a. 1994

    b. 1997

    c. 1995

    d. 1996

8. The Rangers were the first club outside of Canada to win the Stanley Cup.

    a. True

    b. False

9. The franchise was the first to do what in the NHL?

   a. Outfit their jerseys with nameplates
   b. Have a second jersey for away games
   c. Travel by plane
   d. Sound a horn when a player scored a goal

10. Which team did the Rangers defeat to win their first Stanley Cup?

   a. Toronto Maple Leafs
   b. Ottawa Senators
   c. New York Americans
   d. Montreal Maroons

11. The team originally played their home games at Madison Square Garden along with the New York Americans.

   a. True
   b. False

12. How many ex-Rangers have been inducted into the Hockey Hall of Fame player category?

   a. 60
   b. 54
   c. 38
   d. 46

13. How many times did they reach the Stanley Cup Finals in their first 10 years?

   a. 5
   b. 2
   c. 4
   d. 1

14. Frank Boucher was the first coach of the franchise.

    a. True
    b. False

15. In 1943-44, how many games did the Rangers play before securing their first win of the season?

    a. 15
    b. 17
    c. 11
    d. 8

16. How many victories did the club have in its first season?

    a. 31
    b. 27
    c. 22
    d. 25

17. Which team eliminated the Rangers from the playoffs in their first postseason appearance?

    a. Chicago Blackhawks
    b. Boston Bruins
    c. Detroit Cougars
    d. Pittsburgh Pirates

18. What was the highest point total by a player in the Rangers' inaugural season?

    a. 37
    b. 40
    c. 16
    d. 24

19. Which coach has won the most games in franchise history?

    a. Lester Patrick

    b. Alain Vigneault

    c. Emile Francis

    d. Frank Boucher

20. The Rangers beat the Toronto Maple Leafs 5-1 to win their first NHL game.

    a. True

    b. False

QUIZ ANSWERS

1. C – Tex Rickard

2. D – 1927-28

3. A – True

4. C – 59

5. B – 6

6. B – Mike Keenan

7. D – 1996

8. A – True

9. C – Travel by plane

10. D – Montreal Maroons

11. A – True

12. B – 54

13. C – 4

14. B – False

15. A – 15

16. D – 25

17. B – Boston Bruins

18. A – 37

19. C – Emile Francis

20. B – False

DID YOU KNOW?

1. The New York Rangers are based in the borough of Manhattan in New York City, New York. They were founded in 1926 and made their NHL debut in the 1926-27 season. They currently play in the Metropolitan Division of the Eastern Conference. The Buffalo Sabres and New York Islanders are the other NHL teams in New York State. The Rangers are owned by the Madison Square Garden Company.

2. The Rangers are regarded as one of the NHL's Original Six teams and have won the Stanley Cup four times. The team has always played its home games at an arena named Madison Square Garden, which is billed as "the world's most famous arena." The Rangers currently share the rink with the New York Knicks of the National Basketball Association (NBA).

3. There have been four different versions of Madison Square Garden throughout the years. The third was built in 1925, and the Rangers played there until it closed in 1968. The current Madison Square Garden sits above Pennsylvania Station in midtown Manhattan, which means ice level is a good distance above street level. This rink opened in February 1968.

4. George Lewis "Tex" Rickard, who was the president of Madison Square Garden, was the first owner of the

franchise. He was awarded an NHL club in 1926 to help compete with a team known as the New York Americans, who began playing at Madison Square Garden a season earlier. The Americans were quite successful and popular, and Rickard believed a second team in the city would also be a good money-maker.

5. The Rangers were successful right from the get-go as they were crowned American Division Champions in their first NHL season but lost to Boston in the playoffs. Rickard's team was put together by Conn Smythe, who would go on to own the Toronto Maple Leafs. However, Smythe was fired as coach and general manager just before the Rangers' first game and was replaced by Lester Patrick.

6. It took the Rangers nearly no time at all to be crowned Stanley Cup champions as they won the trophy in 1927-28, just their second season in the NHL. They edged the Montreal Maroons three games to two and become the first American NHL club to win the Cup. Forty-four-year-old Lester Patrick played in goal during the series when New York's starting netminder was injured in one of the games.

7. The Rangers were the first NHL club to travel by plane when they flew to Toronto on December 13, 1929. The organization had the Curtiss-Wright Corporation take care of the flight to and from Canada. It didn't help their cause on the ice though as the Maple Leafs edged them 7-6.

8. During the Stanley Cup Finals of 1949-50, the circus came

to town and set up shop at Madison Square Garden. Due to this, the Rangers played all of their home games during the series at Maple Leaf Gardens in Toronto. They went all the way to overtime of the seventh and deciding game before falling to the Detroit Red Wings.

9. In the early 1940s, James E. Norris, who owned the Detroit Red Wings and a major portion of the Chicago Blackhawks, became Madison Square Garden's and the Rangers' largest stockholder. He made sure he didn't take over controlling interest, though, since the NHL's rules stated that a person may not own more than one franchise. Even so, Norris still more or less operated the club to his liking.

10. The Rangers have two minor league affiliates. These are the Hartford Wolf Pack of the American Hockey League (AHL) and the Maine Mariners of the East Coast Hockey League (ECHL). The Rangers' television broadcasts are handled by the Madison Square Garden network, Madison Square Garden Plus, and NBCSN.

CHAPTER 2:

JERSEYS & NUMBERS

QUIZ TIME!

1. What jersey number was the first to be retired by the franchise?

    a. 11
    b. 7
    c. 3
    d. 1

2. How many numbers has the club retired?

    a. 6
    b. 10
    c. 5
    d. 8

3. Goaltender John Davidson is one of only two NHL players to ever wear the number 00.

    a. True
    b. False

4. Who wore number 19 for the team from 2015 to 2017?

   a. Nick Holden
   b. Jesper Fast
   c. Magnus Hellberg
   d. Michael Grabner

5. What number did Rick Nash wear for six seasons?

   a. 60
   b. 27
   c. 61
   d. 42

6. Before Henrik Lundqvist, who was the last goaltender to wear number 30?

   a. Sylvain Blouin
   b. Jason Muzzatti
   c. Mike Dunham
   d. Kirk McLean

7. What New York attraction was featured on the Rangers' alternate jersey from 1996 to 2007?

   a. Statue of Liberty
   b. Broadway Theater
   c. Empire State Building
   d. Chrysler Building

8. The original logo for the team featured a man holding a hockey stick riding a horse but was discarded.

   a. True
   b. False

9. How many alternate jerseys have the Rangers used for special events as of 2019?

    a. 5
    b. 4
    c. 2
    d. 6

10. What year did general manager John Ferguson change the team's jersey to include a shield as the crest?

    a. 1977-78
    b. 1974-75
    c. 1975-76
    d. 1976-77

11. The first time a Ranger wore a number between 60 and 70 was in the 2010s.

    a. True
    b. False

12. Which number has NOT been worn by at least 40 players?

    a. 6
    b. 14
    c. 16
    d. 28

13. Which player currently wears number 76?

    a. Brady Skjei
    b. Anthony DeAngelo
    c. Filip Chytil
    d. Pavel Buchnevich

14. Six different players wore number 22 between 1990 and 2000.

    a. True
    b. False

15. What number did Andy Bathgate wear for three seasons before switching to the number 9?

    a. 12
    b. 15
    c. 37
    d. 63

16. Which number did Anthony Duclair wear in his rookie season?

    a. 64
    b. 85
    c. 63
    d. 44

17. Who was the first player on the Rangers to wear number 38 in 1982?

    a. Tom Younghans
    b. Jeff Bloemberg
    c. Terry Carkner
    d. Robbie Ftorek

18. Which player currently wears number 18?

    a. Chris Kreider
    b. Ryan Strome
    c. Marc Staal
    d. Adam Fox

19. Which number had NOT been retired by the club as of 2019?

    a. 2
    b. 37
    c. 19
    d. 35

20. In 1946-47, the team name on the sweater was fashioned in an arch instead of its normal diagonal pattern.

    a. True
    b. False

QUIZ ANSWERS

1. B – 7

2. D – 8

3. A – True

4. B – Jesper Fast

5. C – 61

6. C – Mike Dunham

7. A – Statue of Liberty

8. A – True

9. B – 4

10. D – 1976-77

11. B – False

12. D – 28

13. A – Brady Skjei

14. B – False

15. A – 12

16. C – 63

17. D – Robbie Ftorek

18. C – Marc Staal

19. B – 37

20. A – True

DID YOU KNOW?

1. The Rangers' jerseys are predominantly dark blue with white and red striping or dark blue with red and white stripes. The team's logo features the word 'Rangers' spelled out on front of the sweater, starting at the top right corner and going downwards in a diagonal fashion. The club has also used alternate jerseys throughout history.

2. The original Rangers jersey was a lighter shade of blue but was changed to the current dark blue back in 1929. The logo was altered in 1946-47 and then changed again the next season. The team has worn red pants since 1929-30. White jerseys were introduced in 1951-52 when the NHL ruled teams needed a different color for home and away games.

3. Between 1998 and 2007, the club also wore an alternate jersey. This featured a logo which was the head of the famous Statue of Liberty with an abbreviated team name of NYR situated below it. The color silver was also used, and this jersey became quite popular with the team's fans.

4. Different versions of Rangers jerseys were also used for special games, such as the 2012 NHL Winter Classic, 2014 NHL Stadium Series, and the 2018 NHL Winter Classic. In addition, Heritage Jerseys were introduced in 2010-11. These were worn against other Original Six teams and on Saturday home games but were retired in 2017-18.

5. Eight jersey numbers have been retired by the Rangers to honor 10 players. These are: Eddie Giacomin (1), Brian Leetch (2), Harry Howell (3), Rod Gilbert (7), Andy Bathgate and Adam Graves (9), Vic Hadfield and Mark Messier (11), Jean Ratelle (19), and Mike Richter (35). And let's not forget former Ranger Wayne Gretzky had his number 99 retired by the NHL.

6. The most popular jersey numbers with Rangers players have been 6 and 14, as 45 different players have worn them. Those who donned number 6 include Eddie Shack, Syl Apps, Mike Tinordi, and Hall-of-Famer Bryan Hextall. Number 14 was once worn by the likes of Pat Hickey, Don Murdoch, Theoren Fleury, and Hall-of-Famers Doug Bentley, Brendan Shanahan, and Jean Ratelle.

7. The lowest number worn by a Ranger is 00, which was the jersey goaltender John Davidson chose. He wore these double digits with the team in 1978. The NHL later banned the number in 1995. Davidson is currently the president of the New York Rangers and was honored by the Hockey Hall of Fame as a broadcaster with the Foster Hewitt Memorial Award in 2009.

8. The highest number worn by any Ranger has been 99, which was taken by Wayne Gretzky from 1997 to 1999. The number 97 was worn by Matt Gilroy from 2010 to 2013. The only number in the 90s that hasn't been worn by a Ranger as of yet is number 98.

9. Every jersey number between 00 and 51 has been worn by at least one Rangers player. In addition, 35 numbers

between 53 and 99 have been worn at least once. The most popular of these has been 55, as seven different Rangers have donned it. These were: Marty McSorley, Igor Ulanov, David Liffiton, Christian Backman, Chris Summers, Nick Holden, and Ryan Lindgren.

10. Eight different Rangers have worn the number 13, even though it's considered to be unlucky in many cultures around the world. Those who tempted fate by wearing it so far have been: Jack Stoddard, Bob Brooke, Sergei Nemchinov, Valeri Kamensky, Richard Scott, Nikolai Zherdev, Daniel Carcillo, and Kevin Hayes.

CHAPTER 3:

FAMOUS QUOTES

QUIZ TIME!

1. Which goaltender said, "How would you like a job where, every time you make a mistake, a big red light goes on and 18,000 people boo?"

    a. Jacques Plante
    b. Henrik Lundqvist
    c. Ed Giacomin
    d. Ron Greschner

2. Who was happy to win the Norris Trophy and stated, "…because I expect it's going to belong to Bobby Orr from now on."?

    a. Barry Beck
    b. Jim Neilson
    c. Harry Howell
    d. Arnie Brown

3. Before working with the team, general manager Glen Sather once remarked, "If I had the Rangers' payroll I'd never lose a game."

a. True

b. False

4. Who stated, "Last time I was starstruck was when I met Roger Federer."?

   a. Rick Nash

   b. J.T. Miller

   c. Brady Skjei

   d. Henrik Lundqvist

5. Which player remarked, "I guarantee we'll win tonight," before the team played Game 6 of the 1994 Eastern Conference Final?

   a. Sergei Zubov

   b. Alex Kovalev

   c. Brian Leetch

   d. Mark Messier

6. Which teammates was Vic Hadfield referring to when he said, "Just a couple of old ladies who can't stop talking."?

   a. Ed Giacomin and Gilles Villemure

   b. Jean Ratelle and Rod Gilbert

   c. Rod Seiling and Jim Neilson

   d. Ed Giacomin and Terry Sawchuk

7. Which Hall-of-Famer once said, "Play with passion and heart. If you don't carry passion into sport—or into any job for that matter—you won't succeed."?

   a. Mike Gartner

   b. Buddy O'Connor

c. Phil Esposito

d. Clint Smith

8. When questioned if hockey fights were real, Ryan McDonagh said, "If they weren't, I'd get in more of them."

a. True

b. False

9. What was Mats Zuccarello talking about when he said, "…you feel like you're the best person, best player in the world. Every conversation you're in, you're like, 'Damn, I'm good.'"?

a. Being an NHL superstar

b. Joining a new team

c. The trade market

d. Free agency

10. Which player was welcomed by the organization with this comment, "So, not only are we getting a great player, we're getting a guy that's got an electric personality… And that's something we needed."?

a. Ryan Strome

b. Filip Chytil

c. Artemi Panarin

d. Kaapo Kakko

11. Coach David Quinn said this about healthy scratch Marc Staal in 2018-19: "We need veterans and we need guys that have been in the league for a while, and I'm expecting him to get back to the level that he needs to get to."

a. True

b. False

12. Which Ranger said, "No matter what line you're playing on, if you bring to the table what you were brought here for, I think we'll be successful."?

a. Chris Kreider

b. Ryan Strome

c. Henrik Lundqvist

d. Mika Zibanejad

13. After Carl Hagelin took a penalty late in a game, which Rangers coach stated, "I focus on the dumbness of Hagelin… He played a hell of a game but that's all washed off from dumbness."?

a. Alain Vigneault

b. John Tortorella

c. David Quinn

d. Tom Renney

14. When asked what his name is for his coffee orders, Artemi Panarin stated, "If I tell them, 'Artemi'…no chance. I just tell them 'John' every time."

a. True

b. False

15. After being informed his leg may have to be amputated, who said, "Not only was my hockey career in doubt, but there was a chance I might leave the hospital with one leg missing—if I left at all."?

a. Dean Prentice
b. Jean Ratelle
c. Rod Gilbert
d. Bun Cook

16. Which former Ranger reminisced about his early playing career, "I played one game a year indoors. That would be the championship."?

    a. Ron Murphy
    b. Dean Prentice
    c. Andy Bathgate
    d. Neil Strain

17. Which Ranger commented, "It's not necessarily the amount of time you spend at practice that counts; it's what you put into the practice."?

    a. Jaromir Jagr
    b. Eric Lindros
    c. Martin St. Louis
    d. Sergei Zubov

18. What was rookie Kaapo Kakko's response to a regression in his play midway through the season?

    a. "Things will turn around."
    b. "I'll do better."
    c. "It sucks that I can't help my teammates more."
    d. "Hockey isn't much fun for me right now."

19. Who said, "Eighteen years ago, my left knee I hurt. I've never had a knee injury in the pros."?

a. Wayne Gretzky
b. Ryan Callahan
c. Brian Leetch
d. Chris Drury

20. Netminder Ed Giacomin came up with, "Goaltending beats top notch scoring anytime!"

a. True
b. False

QUIZ ANSWERS

1. A – Jacques Plante
2. C – Harry Howell
3. A – True
4. D – Henrik Lundqvist
5. D – Mark Messier
6. A – Ed Giacomin and Gilles Villemure
7. C – Phil Esposito
8. B – False
9. D – Free agency
10. C – Artemi Panarin
11. A – True
12. B – Ryan Strome
13. B – John Tortorella
14. A – True
15. C – Rod Gilbert
16. C – Andy Bathgate
17. B – Eric Lindros
18. D – "Hockey isn't much fun for me right now."
19. C – Brian Leetch
20. A – True

DID YOU KNOW?

1. One of the most famous quotes in hockey history was simply "I guarantee we'll win tonight." It came from the mouth of Rangers captain Mark Messier in the 1994 playoffs when his team was down 3-2 in games to New Jersey. The words were splashed all over the headlines in New York newspapers, and Messier backed them up by scoring a hat trick on the road in a 4-2 win. New York beat the Devils in seven games and went on to win the Stanley Cup.

2. When explaining to the media why he was so successful, the NHL's all-time leading scorer and former Ranger Wayne Gretzky remarked, "I don't skate to where the puck is, I skate to where it's going to be."

3. Known for his gentlemanly play and the lack of penalty minutes during his amazing career, Wayne Gretzky was also quoted as saying, "Sometimes people ask, 'Are hockey fights real?' I say, 'If they weren't, I'd get in more of them.'"

4. When Wayne Gretzky retired as a member of the Rangers, NHL Commissioner Gary Bettman told him, "When you take off that sweater, your jersey, after today's game, you will be the last player in the NHL to ever wear 99. You have always been, and you will always be 'The Great One,' and there will never be another."

5. Former Philadelphia Flyers power forward Tim Kerr was a power-play specialist who scored 50 goals a season more than once. He was a handful in front of the net, and those sentiments were echoed by Rangers blueliner Ron Greschner when he said, "Trying to keep him out of the crease is like trying to tackle a Jaguar. Not the animal, the car."

6. Goaltender Gump Worsley, who played the first decade of his NHL career with the Rangers, was one of the very last goaltenders to wear a mask. When a member of the press remarked how dangerous it was to play without one, Worsley replied, "The only worse job is a javelin catcher at a track and field meet."

7. Harry Howell was the anchor of the Rangers' blue line for 17 seasons. When the Hall-of-Famer was named the NHL's best defender for 1966-67, he said, "I'm glad I won the Norris Trophy now, because I expect it's going to belong to Bobby Orr from now on." Orr then won the trophy a record eight years in a row.

8. After the Rangers were eliminated from the playoffs one season, disappointed General Manager Neil Smith was quoted as saying, "The playoffs separate the men from the boys, and we found out we have a lot of boys in our dressing room."

9. Brian Leetch, the Rangers' Hall of Fame defenseman, said, "I didn't know as a rookie coming in how long I'd play in this league, so to play this long is the thing I'm most proud

of." Leetch broke into the NHL in 1977-78 and played until 2005-06.

10. Former head coach John Tortorella came up with hundreds of memorable quotes and was sometimes fined by the NHL for them. When asked why he didn't use Carl Hagelin on the power-play in a game in 2013, the coach stated, "Because he stinks on the power play. He stinks. I don't know why. I wish I could put him on the power play, but every time I put him on, he stinks."

CHAPTER 4:

CATCHY NICKNAMES

QUIZ TIME!

1. What other name do the New York Rangers go by?

   a. The Broadway Boys

   b. The Rowdy Rangers

   c. The Blueshirts

   d. Boys in Blue

2. Who was the "Albanian Assassin"?

   a. Kris King

   b. Joe Cirella

   c. Adam Graves

   d. Tie Domi

3. Under the ownership of Tex Rickard, the Rangers were given the name "Tex's Rangers."

   a. True

   b. False

4. Which famous Ranger is known simply as "The King"?

a. Wayne Gretzky

b. Henrik Lundqvist

c. Mark Messier

d. Mike Richter

5. Which of the following was John Vanbiesbrouck's nickname?

a. Brock

b. Vany

c. Beezer

d. B-Rock

6. Which player was known as the "Russian Rocket"?

a. Roman Lyashenko

b. Artemi Panarin

c. Pavel Bure

d. Alex Kovalev

7. Kjell Samuelsson was given which nickname because of his height?

a. Skyscraper

b. The Hobbit

c. Pony Boy

d. The Human Tripod

8. Gilles Gratton's nickname was "Gratoony the Loony."

a. True

b. False

9. Jesper Fast has what "fast" synonym as his nickname?

a. Speedster

b. Quickie

c. Bolts

d. Quickster

10. In his brief stint with the club, Todd Harvey earned what nickname for his hard work?

a. The Pulse

b. Hustler

c. Heartbeat

d. Workhorse

11. Jim Krulicki was known as the "Polish Prince."

a. True

b. False

12. Who was called the "Little Ball of Hate"?

a. Ken Gernander

b. Ray Ferraro

c. Glenn Healy

d. Pat Verbeek

13. Glenn Healy called which player "Big Ball of Hate"?

a. Ray Ferraro

b. Chris Ferraro

c. Peter Ferraro

d. Jeff Beukeboom

14. Marc Staal's nickname is "Staalsie."

a. True

b. False

15. Ryan McDonagh went by which nickname?

    a. Donut
    b. The Bulldozer
    c. Mac Truck
    d. 18-Wheeler

16. Luc Robitaille shared the nickname "Lucky" with which other Ranger?

    a. Shane Churla
    b. Bruce Driver
    c. Brian Leetch
    d. Pierre Larouche

17. Which player had the nickname "The Flower"?

    a. Phil Esposito
    b. Guy Lafleur
    c. Jim Neilson
    d. Jerry Butler

18. Don Murdoch had which violent nickname?

    a. Murder
    b. Killer
    c. Hitman
    d. Headhunter

19. What is Artemi Panarin's food related nickname?

    a. Breadman
    b. Muffin Man
    c. Captain Cupcake
    d. Pancake

20. Mark Messier was known as "The Bull."

    a. True

    b. False

QUIZ ANSWERS

1. C – The Blueshirts

2. D – Tie Domi

3. A – True

4. B – Henrik Lundqvist

5. C – Beezer

6. C – Pavel Bure

7. D – The Human Tripod

8. A – True

9. B – Quickie

10. C – Heartbeat

11. B – False

12. D – Pat Verbeek

13. A – Ray Ferraro

14. B – False

15. C – Mac Truck

16. D – Pierre Larouche

17. B – Guy Lafleur

18. A – Murder

19. A – Breadman

20. B – False

DID YOU KNOW?

1. New York City typically goes by the nickname "The Big Apple," while Madison Square Garden is generally referred to as "MSG." As for the Rangers team, it's basically known collectively as "The Blueshirts." However, the club was also nicknamed "The Broadway Blueshirts" in the early years when Madison Square Garden was located on 48th Street, close to Times Square.

2. Goaltender Lorne Worsley was simply known as "Gump" throughout his Hall of Fame career because of his resemblance to a comic strip character named Gump. He was the NHL's rookie of the year with the Rangers in 1952-53. He played 10 years with the team and retired from hockey in 1973-74 due to a fear of flying. Worsley wore a mask for just the final six games of his career.

3. Emile Francis was well known for his association with the Rangers. He played for the team from 1948 to 1952, then coached the squad between 1965 and 1975, and also served as the club's general manager. The former goaltender, who was just 5 feet 5 inches tall and weighed 155 lbs., was nicknamed "Cat" due to his cat-like reflexes when stopping the puck.

4. Frederick Joseph Cook was better known as "Bun" Cook to hockey fans. Cook played left wing on the Rangers' "Bread Line" with Frank Boucher and his brother Bill

Cook and helped the team win two Stanley Cups. The Hall-of-Famer was nicknamed "Bun" by a sportswriter who said Cook was as "quick as a bunny" when playing hockey.

5. The late 1960s and early '70s Rangers' trio of wingers Rod Gilbert, Vic Hadfield, and center Jean Ratelle was known as the "GAG Line." This stood for 'goal a game' as the fans felt they could rely on the line to score at least once an outing. In 1971-72, Ratelle placed third in NHL scoring, while Hadfield finished fourth and Gilbert fifth.

6. Rangers enforcer Tie Domi actually had two nicknames. "Tie" itself was a moniker since his given name is Tahir. In addition, he was also known as the "Albanian Assassin" due to his heritage. Domi was well known for dropping the gloves and recorded 3,515 penalty minutes in 1,020 games with 238 minutes in 98 playoff contests. He had 526 of those minutes in 82 regular-season games as a Ranger from 1990-91 to 1992-93.

7. Former Montreal Canadiens star winger Bernie Geoffrion spent the final two seasons of his playing career with the Rangers from 1966 to 1968. He then coached the club in 1968-69 for 42 games before resigning due to health problems. Geoffrion was known as "Boom Boom" for the ferocity of his slapshot, which he also claimed to have invented.

8. Hall of Fame winger Guy Lafleur was another ex-Montreal Canadiens Hall-of-Famer who played with the Rangers

near the end of his career. He skated in the 1988-89 campaign and posted 45 points in 65 games. He's also another player who had two nicknames. Lafleur was basically known as "The Flower" to English-speaking fans, while French-speaking supporters knew him as "Le Demon Blond."

9. Two Rangers Hall-of-Famers shared the nickname "Babe." Blueliner Walter Peter Pratt was known as "Babe" Pratt throughout his playing days and helped the team win the Stanley Cup in 1940. Also, defenseman/forward Charles Albert Siebert went by the name "Babe," and he helped the squad hoist the Cup in 1932-33.

10. Alf Pike was a versatile forward who played with the Rangers from 1939 to 1947 and scored some big goals in the 1939-40 playoffs to help the team capture the Stanley Cup. Since Pike was a licensed mortician and worked his craft in the offseason, he was known as "The Embalmer." Pike also coached the Rangers between 1959 and 1961.

CHAPTER 5:

THE CAPTAIN CLASS

QUIZ TIME!

1. Who was the captain of the club during the 1967 NHL expansion era?

   a. Andy Bathgate
   b. Camille Henry
   c. Vic Hadfield
   d. Bob Nevin

2. How many captains have the Rangers had through the first 93 seasons?

   a. 25
   b. 19
   c. 30
   d. 27

3. Bill Cook was the franchise's first captain.

   a. True
   b. False

4. What is the highest point total recorded by a captain as of 2019?

   a. 106
   b. 96
   c. 107
   d. 99

5. How many penalty minutes did captain Barry Beck record in the 1980-81 season?

   a. 244
   b. 231
   c. 196
   d. 206

6. Which Ranger was captain from 1957 to 1961?

   a. Eddie Shack
   b. Harry Howell
   c. Red Sullivan
   d. Andy Bathgate

7. What is the lowest plus/minus recorded by a Rangers captain?

   a. -38
   b. -27
   c. -41
   d. -36

8. Mark Messier held the captaincy the longest at 10 years.

   a. True
   b. False

9. Who was the youngest captain of the Rangers at 22 years old?

    a. Ron Duguay
    b. Dave Maloney
    c. Mike McEwen
    d. Don Maloney

10. In 2006-07, how many points did Jaromir Jagr score?

    a. 93
    b. 100
    c. 88
    d. 96

11. As of the 2019-20 season, the Rangers do not have a primary captain.

    a. True
    b. False

12. Which player was the oldest to hold the captaincy?

    a. Mark Messier
    b. Bill Cook
    c. Jaromir Jagr
    d. Phil Esposito

13. Who was NOT one of the alternate captains on the 2019-20 roster?

    a. Mika Zibanejad
    b. Chris Kreider
    c. Jesper Fast
    d. Brendan Smith

14. Vic Hadfield currently holds the best plus/minus of any Rangers captain, with a +60 in a season.

    a. True
    b. False

15. Who was NOT named team captain in the 1980-81 season?

    a. Dave Maloney
    b. Phil Esposito
    c. Barry Beck
    d. Walt Tkaczuk

16. Who was captain for just one season, which was 1949-50?

    a. Frank Eddolls
    b. Jaromir Jagr
    c. Buddy O'Connor
    d. Wayne Gretzky

17. Which player was the captain from 2014 to 2018?

    a. Mats Zuccarello
    b. Marc Staal
    c. Ryan Callahan
    d. Ryan McDonagh

18. How many points did captain Chris Drury score in the 2008-09 playoffs?

    a. 9
    b. 5
    c. 7
    d. 1

19. Who was the captain when the club won their third Stanley Cup?

    a. Bill Cook
    b. Art Coulter
    c. Ott Heller
    d. Neil Colville

20. Red Sullivan played all 70 games in every season he was captain.

    a. True
    b. False

QUIZ ANSWERS

1. D – Bob Nevin

2. D – 27

3. A – True

4. C – 107

5. B – 231

6. C – Red Sullivan

7. A – -38

8. B – False

9. B – Dave Maloney

10. D – 96

11. A – True

12. A – Mark Messier

13. D – Brendan Smith

14. A – True

15. B – Phil Esposito

16. C – Buddy O'Connor

17. D – Ryan McDonagh

18. D – 1

19. B – Art Coulter

20. A – True

DID YOU KNOW?

1. The Rangers have had 27 different captains since the club's inception. The first was Bill Cook in 1926-27, with the last being Ryan McDonagh up to 2017-18. However, when McDonagh was traded to the Tampa Bay Lightning in February 2018, the club never filled the position. As of the conclusion of the 2019-20 campaign, the team dressed alternate captains instead of a captain.

2. Of the club's 27 skippers, 11 of them were inducted into the Hockey Hall of Fame. These are: Bill Cook, Art Coulter, Neil Colville, Buddy O'Connor, Allan Stanley, Harry Howell, Andy Bathgate, Brad Park, Phil Esposito, Mark Messier, and Brian Leetch. In addition, Jaromir Jagr is a certainty to be enshrined when he's eligible.

3. The youngest captain in team annals was Dave Maloney at the age of 22, while Mark Messier was the oldest at 43. Messier had two stints as captain with the first being from 1991-92 to 1996-97. Brian Leetch took over for the next three seasons when Messier signed for Vancouver as a free agent. Messier then wore the C from 2000-01 to 2003-04 when he returned to New York in 2000 as a free agent.

4. The longest-serving captain was Bill Cook who held the position from 1926-27 to 1936-37 for a total of 11 consecutive seasons. The Hall of Fame winger played his entire 475-game NHL career with the Blueshirts and

notched 228 goals and 388 points with 13 goals and 24 points in 46 playoff games. He rarely missed a game, led the league in goals twice, and won two Stanley Cups.

5. The shortest stint as captain belongs to unheralded two-way center Walt Tkaczuk as he wore the C for 43 games in 1980-81. He played with the team for his entire NHL career from 1967 to 1981 and posted 678 points in 945 games and 51 points in 93 playoff matches. Tkaczuk suffered an eye injury February 2, 1981, and never played again.

6. The most physical Rangers captain was defenseman Barry Beck. He served over 100 minutes in penalties the first four seasons he wore the C. Beck recorded 231 minutes in his first year as captain and close to 700 minutes in his stint, which lasted from 1980-81 to 1985-86. He also chipped in with 180 points during that time.

7. The best point-scoring season by a captain was in 1991-92 when Mark Messier notched 35 goals and 75 assists for 107 points. Vic Hadfield was right behind him as he tallied 50 goals and 56 assists for 106 points in 1971-72. Hadfield was the only Ranger to reach 50 goals in a season while acting as Rangers captain. He was also a +60 that year.

8. Hall-of-Famer Ott Heller was the Rangers' third captain as he held the post from 1942 to 1945. He started his career as a right winger and then moved to the blue line. Heller played with the squad from 1931-32 to 1945-46 and won two Stanley Cups with the team. He co-led the Rangers in

penalty minutes in 1936-37 with 49 and led in assists in 1938-39 with 23.

9. Buddy O'Connor was a Hall of Fame center who captained the team for just one season in 1949-50 when he scored 11 goals and 33 points in 66 games. He played the first six years of his career with Montreal and the last four with the Rangers from 1947 to 1951. He won the Lady Byng and Hart Trophies in his first season with New York, with 60 points in 60 games. This made O'Connor the first player to win both awards in the same season, and he was named Canada's athlete of the year for his performance.

10. One of the Rangers' most low-key captains was Kelly Kisio between 1987-88 and 1990-91. The center played in the Big Apple for five seasons after being acquired in a July 1986 trade with Detroit. The team then lost him to Minnesota in the 1991 NHL Expansion Draft. In between, Kisio notched 305 points in 336 games with the Rangers, with 415 minutes in penalties.

CHAPTER 6:

STATISTICALLY SPEAKING

QUIZ TIME!

1. What is the most goals scored in a season by a Ranger?

   a. 60

   b. 54

   c. 57

   d. 46

2. What was Henrik Lundqvist's save percentage in the 2013-14 playoffs?

   a. .934

   b. .925

   c. .927

   d. .931

3. As of 2019-20, the Rangers have finished 10 seasons with at least 100 points.

   a. True

   b. False

4. In 1962-63, who had a 10-game goal-scoring streak?

    a. Camille Henry
    b. Earl Ingarfield
    c. Doug Harvey
    d. Andy Bathgate

5. Which Rangers goalie posted a club-record 13 shutouts in a season?

    a. Ed Giacomin
    b. Lorne Chabot
    c. John Ross Roach
    d. Henrik Lundqvist

6. How many goals did the Rangers score in their inaugural season?

    a. 103
    b. 94
    c. 88
    d. 75

7. Which player led the team in points with 73 in the 1984-85 season?

    a. Rejio Ruotsalainen
    b. Mike Rogers
    c. Tomas Sandstrom
    d. Anders Hedberg

8. Wayne Gretzky scored a total of nine goals in his final season with the Rangers.

    a. True
    b. False

9. Who has recorded the most assists in a season?

    a. Wayne Gretzky
    b. Jaromir Jagr
    c. Brian Leetch
    d. Sergei Zubov

10. How many assists a game did Jean Ratelle average in 1971-72?

    a. 0.83
    b. 0.79
    c. 0.98
    d. 1.00

11. Tie Domi had the most penalty minutes in a season for the club.

    a. True
    b. False

12. Brad Richards and which other player scored nine game-winning goals in 2011-12?

    a. Carl Hagelin
    b. Derek Stepan
    c. Ryan Callahan
    d. Marian Gaborik

13. In 2017-18, what was the highest hit total by a player on the team?

    a. 127
    b. 145
    c. 130
    d. 138

14. The highest plus/minus recorded in a season is +63 in 1971-72.

    a. True
    b. False

15. How many players tallied over 15 points in the 1993-94 playoffs?

    a. 3
    b. 6
    c. 4
    d. 7

16. Which player had a team-low -17 in 1999-2000?

    a. Valeri Kamensky
    b. Adam graves
    c. Brian Leetch
    d. Mike York

17. How many shots did Gump Worsley face in 1955-56?

    a. 2,677
    b. 2,702
    c. 2,574
    d. 2,355

18. Bill Cook averaged how many goals per game in 1926-27?

    a. 0.63
    b. 0.75
    c. 0.58
    d. 0.77

19. What is the most games a Rangers goalie has played in a season?

    a. 66
    b. 72
    c. 74
    d. 73

20. The most wins by a Blueshirts netminder in a season is 42.

    a. True
    b. False

QUIZ ANSWERS

1. B – 54

2. C – .927

3. A – True

4. D – Andy Bathgate

5. C – John Ross Roach

6. B – 94

7. A – Rejio Ruotsalainen

8. A – True

9. C – Brian Leetch

10. D – 1.00

11. B – False

12. C – Ryan Callahan

13. C – 130

14. A – True

15. B – 6

16. D – Mike York

17. C – 2,574

18. B – 0.75

19. D – 73

20. A – True

DID YOU KNOW?

1. The most points the Rangers earned in a season was 113, with a record of 53-22-7—with the 53 wins also being a club record. Their points percentage that year was .689, which was third best in team annals. They posted a team-high .699 points percentage in both 1970-71 and 1971-72 when they took 109 of a possible 140 points in 70 games each season.

2. The worst points total for a Rangers squad was just 17 in 1943-44, with a record of 6-39-5. Their points percentage that 50-game season was also their lowest ever at .170. They finished last place in the six-team NHL that season as they did each year from 1942-43 to 1945-46 and again in 1948-49.

3. When the 2019-20 regular season concluded, the Rangers' all-time record (wins-losses-ties-overtime losses) stood at 2856-2693-808-147 for 6,667 points. They had made the playoffs 59 times as of 2018-19, with a record of 244-263, with four Stanley Cups to their name.

4. On an individual regular-season basis, winger Rod Gilbert is the all-time goal-scoring king with 406 and also leads in points with 1,021. Defender Brian Leetch earned the most assists at 741, while blueliner Harry Howell played the most games at 1,160. Rearguard Ron Greschner was assessed the most penalty minutes at 1,226. Winger Camille Henry is tops with 116 power-play goals.

5. The top playoff point-getter for the team is Brian Leetch, with 89, and he also leads in assists at 61. The most postseason goals were scored by Rod Gilbert, with 34, while Adam Graves has a team-best 13 on the power-play. As for games played, netminder Henrik Lundqvist had appeared in 128 playoff contests at the end of 2018-19, while the most played by a skater was 122 by defenseman Dan Girardi.

6. When it comes to goalies, Henrik Lundqvist had the most wins with 459, the most shutouts at 64, and had played the most games at 887. He led the team in most playoff games at 128, most wins with 61, and the most shutouts with 10. Lundqvist holds the single-season records for games played at 73 and save percentage with .930. Let's add that he leads the team all-time in goals against, minutes, losses, shots against, saves, and save percentage at .918.

7. Offensively, forward Jaromir Jagr recorded the most goals and points in a season in 2005-06 when he scored 54 goals and 123 points, respectively. He also took a team-record 368 shots on net that campaign. Meanwhile, defenseman Brian Leetch tallied the most assists in a season with 80 in 1991-92.

8. Considering clutch scoring, Rod Gilbert's 52 game-winning goals in the regular season is the team record, while Butch Keeling, Brian Leetch, and Cecil Dion each scored seven overtime markers in the regular season. And even though Mark Messier was known for his production, he was a fine penalty-killer as he notched a record 23 shorthanded goals with the Rangers.

9. Checking out the top players per game, Jaromir Jagr's 1.15 points per contest is the all-time career regular-season best. Goals per game belongs to Pat Verbeek at 0.58, while Wayne Gretzky earned the most assists per outing at 0.82. Ulf Nilsson was the most accurate regular-season shooter with a 22.2 shooting percentage.

10. The official plus/minus statistic wasn't introduced by the NHL until 1967-68. However, center Walt Tkaczuk had a career best in the regular season at +184. The worst rating belongs to Earl Ingarfield at -117. Perhaps surprisingly, fellow center Phil Esposito holds the second-worst mark at -116. The best mark in the regular season was posted by defender Brad Park with +63 in 1971-72.

CHAPTER 7:

THE TRADE MARKET

QUIZ TIME!

1. Tough guy Nick Fotiu was acquired by the Hartford Whalers in exchange for what trade package?

    a. 5th round draft pick

    b. 4th and 5th round draft picks

    c. Cash and future considerations

    d. 3rd round draft pick

2. The Rangers traded Chris Higgins and Ales Kotalik for which two players in 2010?

    a. Brandon Prust and Curtis Glencross

    b. Adam Pardy and Olli Jokinen

    c. Olli Jokinen and Brandon Prust

    d. Dustin Boyd and Dave Moss

3. In 2015, the Rangers traded Cam Talbot for fellow netminder Antti Raanta.

    a. True

    b. False

4. The Rangers acquired enforcer John Scott for a 5th round draft pick. How many games did he play in New York?

    a. 40
    b. 6
    c. 18
    d. 179

5. Who did the club trade to the Ottawa Senators for Mika Zibanejad?

    a. Anthony Duclair
    b. Michael Grabner
    c. Derick Brassard
    d. Derek Stepan

6. Which player did the Rangers NOT receive when trading J.T. Miller and Ryan McDonagh to the Tampa Bay Lightning?

    a. Brett Howden
    b. Libor Hajek
    c. Vladislav Namestnikov
    d. Darren Raddysh

7. The Rangers traded Larry Brown for which defenseman in 1970?

    a. Pete Stemkowski
    b. Arnie Brown
    c. Ron Harris
    d. Gerry Hart

8. The club traded defender Keith Yandle to the Florida Panthers in exchange for 4th and 6th round draft picks.

a. True

b. False

9. Which team did the Rangers pick up Mike Gartner from?

    a. Phoenix Coyotes

    b. Toronto Maple Leafs

    c. Minnesota North Stars

    d. Washington Capitals

10. Who did the Rangers NOT receive from the Toronto Maple Leafs in 1964?

    a. Bob Nevin

    b. Don McKenney

    c. Arnie Brown

    d. Bill Collins

11. The Blueshirts swapped Anson Carter for Jaromir Jagr in 2004.

    a. True

    b. False

12. How many trades did the team make in 2000-01?

    a. 5

    b. 12

    c. 8

    d. 11

13. Who did the Rangers receive in return for Ryan Callahan and a 1st and 2nd round draft pick from Tampa Bay?

    a. Ryan Malone

    b. Teddy Purcell

c. Martin St. Louis

d. Cody Kunyk

14. Seven-year Rangers netminder Dave Kerr was acquired by the club for cash.

a. True

b. False

15. Which team did the franchise make their first trade with?

a. New York Americans

b. Montreal Maroons

c. Boston Bruins

d. Toronto St. Patricks

16. The Rangers traded Scott Gomez to which club in 2009?

a. San Jose Sharks

b. Montreal Canadiens

c. New Jersey Devils

d. Florida Panthers

17. How many points did Luc Robitaille score after being traded to the Los Angeles Kings in 1997?

a. 48

b. 40

c. 88

d. 74

18. Who was NOT sent to New York by the Boston Bruins in exchange for Rick Nash?

a. Brian Gionta

b. Ryan Lindgren

c. Matt Beleskey

d. Ryan Spooner

19. How many goals did Rick Middleton score in his career with Boston after being traded for Ken Hodge?

a. 463

b. 376

c. 402

d. 350

20. Eddie Shack was traded by the Rangers three times in the same season.

a. True

b. False

QUIZ ANSWERS

1. A – 5th round draft pick

2. C – Olli Jokinen and Brandon Prust

3. B – False

4. B – 6

5. C – Derick Brassard

6. D – Darren Raddysh

7. A – Pete Stemkowski

8. A – True

9. C – Minnesota North Stars

10. B – Don McKenney

11. A – True

12. D – 11

13. C – Martin St. Louis

14. A – True

15. D – Toronto St. Patricks

16. B – Montreal Canadiens

17. B – 40

18. A – Brian Gionta

19. C – 402

20. B – False

DID YOU KNOW?

1. After finishing as runner-up in Calder Trophy voting as a rookie two years earlier, the club sent Tony Amonte and Matt Oates to Chicago with seven games left in the 1993-94 campaign. The Rangers received Brian Noonan and Stephane Matteau and won the Stanley Cup that season. However, Amonte would become a star with Chicago and one of the highest-scoring American-born players in history, while both Matteau and Noonan didn't play with the Rangers after 1995-96.

2. Hall of Fame defenseman Brian Leetch was one of the greatest Rangers ever, but the club traded him twice. He was dealt to Edmonton for Jussi Markkanen and a 4th round draft pick in June of 2003 but never left town as he re-signed with New York as a free agent just a month later. Leetch was then traded near the end of the 2003-04 season as a rental player to Toronto for a 1st and 2nd round draft pick.

3. Colorful forward Eddie Shack was another player the Rangers technically swapped twice, and the deals came in the same year. He was dealt to Detroit in February 1960 with Bill Gadsby for Billy McNeil and Red Kelly. However, McNeil and Kelly refused to report to the Blueshirts. The NHL nullified the deal, and Shack was sent to Toronto exactly nine months later for Johnny Wilson and Pat Hannigan.

4. Winger Rick Middleton showed a lot of potential in Manhattan with 90 points in his first 124 games. However, the Rangers dealt the 22-year-old to Boston for 32-year-old Ken Hodge in May 1976. Middleton went on to win the Lady Byng Trophy and post 402 goals and 898 points with the Bruins in 881 games. Hodge scored 68 points in 96 contests with the Rangers before calling it quits.

5. One of the biggest blockbuster trades in Rangers history saw them acquire 33-year-old center Phil Esposito and blueliner Carol Vadnais from Boston for center Jean Ratelle, defender Brad Park, and forward Joe Zanussi. Esposito posted 404 points in 422 games in New York, while Vadnais netted 246 points in 485 contests. Meanwhile, Park accumulated 417 points in 501 games with Boston, Ratelle had 450 points in 419 outings, and Zanussi played just 68 games. Esposito, Park, and Ratelle were all inducted into the Hall of Fame.

6. The Rangers pulled a heist in January 2004 when they acquired legendary forward Jaromir Jagr from Washington for winger Anson Carter. Jagr would score 319 points with the Rangers in 277 games, with 27 points in 23 playoff outings. He also set the franchise scoring mark with 123 points in 2005-06. Carter had played just 54 times for the Rangers, with 22 points. Washington then traded him to Los Angeles for Jared Aulin just six weeks after acquiring him from New York.

7. When Eric Lindros refused to sign with the Quebec Nordiques after being drafted 1st overall in 1991, the NHL

let an arbitrator decide his fate. Quebec caused chaos when they accepted trades from the Rangers and Philadelphia. The arbitrator eventually ruled in favor of Philadelphia as they sent Peter Forsberg, Steve Duchesne, Ron Hextall, Chris Simon, Mike Ricci, Kerry Huffman, two draft picks, and $15 million to Quebec. The Rangers reportedly offered Alexei Kovalev, Tony Amonte, James Patrick, Doug Weight, Mike Richter, or John Vanbiesbrouck, three 1st round draft picks, and $12 million.

8. The Rangers acquired Christopher Higgins, Ryan McDonagh, Pavel Valentenko, and the rights to Doug Janik in June 2009 for Scott Gomez, Tom Pyatt, and Mike Busto. Gomez had five years left on his contract, with $30 million owed to him. It looked like a gamble since blueliner McDonagh had yet to make his NHL debut. He would later captain the team and help them reach the Stanley Cup Finals. Gomez played well in Montreal for a season, but the club eventually bought out his contract.

9. Power forward Rick Nash was grabbed by New York in 2012 from Columbus along with Steve Delisle and a 3rd round draft pick. They had to give up Brandon Dubinsky, Tim Erixon, Artem Anisimov, and their 1st round selection in 2013 though. The trade was evened out somewhat when the Rangers drafted Pavel Buchnevich with the pick they acquired. The 24-year-old had posted 147 points in 247 games with the Blueshirts by the end of the 2019-20 season.

10. With the Rangers last winning the Stanley Cup in 1940, they felt it was time to turn things around when they

made a deal with Edmonton for Mark Messier in November 1991. They acquired Messier and future considerations for Bernie Nicholls, Steven Rice, and Louie DeBrusk. Messier would captain the team for 10 seasons and lead them to the Stanley Cup in 1993-94. He had two stints with the team and notched 691 points in 698 games, with 80 points in 70 playoff matches.

CHAPTER 8:

DRAFT DAY

QUIZ TIME!

1. Which player was selected 4th overall and played only 78 NHL games?

   a. Dan Blackburn

   b. Dylan Reese

   c. Michael Sauer

   d. Pavel Brendl

2. How many selections has the club made in the 1st round as of 2019?

   a. 56

   b. 43

   c. 71

   d. 39

3. Henrik Lundqvist was selected 205th overall in the 2000 Entry Draft.

   a. True

   b. False

4. Which player drafted by the club scored a total of 1,033 points in his NHL career?

    a. Brian Leetch
    b. Rick Middleton
    c. Doug Weight
    d. Alex Kovalev

5. As of 2019, how many 1st overall selections had the franchise made?

    a. 5
    b. 1
    c. 9
    d. 0

6. How many selections did the club make in the 1974 Draft?

    a. 7
    b. 15
    c. 2
    d. 23

7. Which goaltender was drafted 6th overall in 2004?

    a. Dan Blackburn
    b. Antoine Lafleur
    c. Al Montoya
    d. Chris Holt

8. Andre Veilleux, the club's 1st overall pick in 1965, never played an NHL game.

    a. True
    b. False

9. How many blueliners had the franchise drafted as of 2019?

    a. 231
    b. 163
    c. 190
    d. 96

10. Who did the club select 21st overall in 2017?

    a. Olof Lindbom
    b. Brandon Crawley
    c. Lias Andersson
    d. Filip Chytil

11. The Rangers had drafted only 17 goaltenders as of 2019.

    a. True
    b. False

12. What round was goaltender Igor Shesterkin selected in back in 2014?

    a. 4th
    b. 3rd
    c. 6th
    d. 5th

13. How many defensemen were selected in the 1978 Draft?

    a. 4
    b. 10
    c. 2
    d. 7

14. The fewest players the franchise drafted in a season is two.

a. True

b. False

15. Which future Hall-of-Famer did the Rangers select in the 5th round in 1995?

a. Sergei Nemchinov

b. Doug Weight

c. Mattias Norstrom

d. Sergei Zubov

16. Where was Ron Greschner selected in 1974?

a. 6th overall

b. 17th overall

c. 54th overall

d. 32nd overall

17. What year did the Rangers draft Michael Del Zotto, Derek Stepan, and Dale Weise?

a. 2008

b. 2006

c. 2007

d. 2009

18. Who did the Rangers select 2nd overall in 1966?

a. Joey Johnston

b. Andre Dupont

c. Brad Park

d. Robert Dickson

19. How many wingers did the team pick in the 1989 Draft?

a. 7

b. 2

c. 5

d. 9

20. The four players the franchise selected in the first-ever draft never played an NHL game.

a. True

b. False

QUIZ ANSWERS

1. D – Pavel Brendl
2. A – 56
3. A – True
4. C – Doug Weight
5. B – 1
6. D – 23
7. C – Al Montoya
8. A – True
9. B – 163
10. D – Filip Chytil
11. B – False
12. A – 4th
13. D – 7
14. B – False
15. D – Sergei Zubov
16. D – 32nd overall
17. A – 2008
18. C – Brad Park
19. D – 9
20. A – True

DID YOU KNOW?

1. After the 2019 NHL Entry Draft was completed, the Rangers had chosen a total of 528 players since it was introduced in 1963. They have also taken 85 players in the various Supplemental Drafts for American college players between 1986 and 1993 with none of them making an impact on the team and in the NHL.

2. Most of the six NHL teams didn't fare too well in the 1963 Draft, including the Rangers. They selected Al Osborne (4th), Terry Jones (10th), Mike Cummins (15th), and Cam Allison (20th) with their picks, and none of them played a game in the NHL. In addition, two of their picks in 1964 also failed to play a game in the league.

3. The first player drafted by the Rangers to make the NHL was winger Tim Ecclestone who was taken in the 2nd round with the 9th overall pick in 1964. He went on to score 359 points in 692 regular-season games, but none of them came with the Rangers as he was traded to St. Louis in June 1967.

4. The longest-serving NHL player taken by the Rangers in the draft as of the 2019-20 season was winger Alexei Kovalev. He was drafted 15th overall in 1991 and went on to play 1,316 games in the NHL, with 430 goals, 599 assists, and 1,029 points to his name. He played two stints with the team and helped them win the Stanley Cup in 1993-94.

5. Doug Weight was the highest-scoring Ranger ever drafted as he tallied 1,033 points in 1,238 regular-season games. He played just 118 contests with the Rangers though as he was traded to Edmonton in 1993 for Esa Tikkanen after being drafted 34th overall in 1990. Weight also won the Stanley Cup with Carolina in 2006.

6. The most successful NHLer drafted by the Blueshirts was rearguard Brian Leetch. The Hall-of-Famer was selected 9th overall in 1986 and posted 1,028 points in 1,205 career games, with 97 points in 95 playoff contests. Leetch played all but 76 of his games with New York, and the five-time All-Star won a Stanley Cup, the Calder Trophy, the Smythe Trophy, and two James Norris Trophies with the team.

7. As of 2019, the Rangers have drafted 1st overall just once in franchise history. This came when they chose Andre Veilleux with the pick in 1965, and he never played an NHL game. They have drafted 2nd overall on two occasions as winger Kaapo Kakko was taken in 2019, and Brad Park was selected in 1996. Park would go on to enjoy a Hall of Fame career mainly with the Rangers and Boston.

8. The lowest-drafted Ranger to have a successful NHL career was defender Kim Johnsson. He was selected in the 11th round with the 286th pick in 1994, which was the very last choice in the draft. In fact, he's currently the lowest-drafted Ranger ever. Johnsson would play 739 career regular-season games, with 284 points to his name. Just 151 of those contests were in New York though.

9. The highest-drafted goaltenders by the club were George Surmay and Al Montoya. Surmay was taken in the 2nd round with the 6th overall pick in 1965, while Montoya was taken with the 6th selection in the 1st round in 2004. Surmay never played an NHL game, and Montoya played 169 in the league but none with the Rangers. He was traded to Phoenix in a six-player deal in 2008.

10. The lowest-drafted goalie by the Rangers to hit the big time was Henrik Lundqvist who was chosen 205th overall in 2000. Lundqvist was still playing as of 2019-20 and holds several Rangers goaltending records and milestones. Lundqvist is also a two-time All-Star who won the Vezina Trophy in 2011-12. There's a good chance he'll be inducted into the Hall of Fame when he hangs up his skates.

CHAPTER 9:

GOALTENDER TIDBITS

QUIZ TIME!

1. How many regular-season wins had Henrik Lundqvist posted at the end of 2019-20?

   a. 425

   b. 436

   c. 459

   d. 463

2. Who was the club's primary goaltender in their inaugural season?

   a. Hal Winkler

   b. Lorne Chabot

   c. Joe Miller

   d. John Ross Roach

3. Mike Richter played 666 games as a Ranger.

   a. True

   b. False

4. How many saves did Ed Giacomin make in 1968-69?

    a. 1,765
    b. 1,916
    c. 1,717
    d. 1,363

5. Ken McAuley recorded how many losses in 1943-44?

    a. 26
    b. 19
    c. 41
    d. 39

6. Which goaltender had a goals-against average of 1.41, the best in a single season?

    a. Mike Richter
    b. John Ross Roach
    c. Gilles Villemure
    d. Dave Kerr

7. What was Gump Worsley's save percentage average in his 10 years with the club?

    a. .912
    b. .903
    c. .913
    d. .915

8. Coach Lester Patrick acted as an emergency backup goalie for the club in their 1927-28 playoff run.

    a. True
    b. False

9. How many goaltenders played at least one game in 2009-10?

    a. 6
    b. 7
    c. 4
    d. 5

10. How many games did Martin Biron play with the club in 2010-11?

    a. 18
    b. 13
    c. 17
    d. 20

11. John Vanbiesbrouck played 500 games for the Rangers.

    a. True
    b. False

12. What was Mike Richter's save percentage in the 1993-94 playoffs?

    a. .918
    b. .941
    c. .927
    d. .921

13. Which goaltender did NOT record exactly 24 shutouts with the team?

    a. Gump Worsley
    b. Chuck Rayner
    c. John Vanbiesbrouck
    d. Mike Richter

14. The most career penalty minutes recorded by a Rangers goalie is 242.

    a. True
    b. False

15. In 93 seasons, how many goaltenders have played at least one game for the club?

    a. 90
    b. 86
    c. 77
    d. 50

16. In 1943, Bill Beveridge allowed how many goals in 17 games played?

    a. 64
    b. 27
    c. 89
    d. 33

17. What is the most saves made in a season by one goaltender?

    a. 2,079
    b. 2,224
    c. 2,306
    d. 2,376

18. Which is the highest point total by a Rangers netminder in their career as of 2019?

    a. 21
    b. 19

c. 26

d. 28

19. How many games did prospect Igor Shesterkin win in his first 12 games played with the club?

    a. 10

    b. 9

    c. 12

    d. 11

20. Henrik Lundqvist ranked second in wins among active goaltenders as of 2019.

    a. True

    b. False

QUIZ ANSWERS

1. C – 459

2. B – Lorne Chabot

3. A – True

4. A – 1,765

5. D – 39

6. B – John Ross Roach

7. C – .913

8. A – True

9. D – 5

10. C – 17

11. B – False

12. D – .921

13. C – John Vanbiesbrouck

14. B – False

15. B – 86

16. C – 89

17. D – 2,376

18. D – 28

19. A – 10

20. A – True

DID YOU KNOW?

1. A total of seven former goaltenders who played with the Rangers franchise are enshrined in the Hockey Hall of Fame. These are: Eddie Giacomin, Johnny Bower, Terry Sawchuk, Harry Lumley, Jacques Plante, Chuck Rayner, and Gump Worsley. In addition, former player, coach, and general manager Emile Francis was inducted as a builder.

2. In the Rangers' second season, they beat the Montreal Maroons in five games to hoist the Stanley Cup. With neither team dressing a backup goalie, 44-year-old Rangers head coach Lester Patrick found himself between the posts for the final two periods of the second game. Starter Lorne Chabot had to leave with an eye injury, and Montreal's head coach wouldn't allow NHL goalie Alex Connell to play since he didn't belong to the Rangers. Patrick allowed one goal, and New York won the encounter in overtime.

3. Netminder Dan Blackburn was drafted 10th overall by the Blueshirts in 2001 and looked to be a top prospect. In the summer of 2003, he suffered a shoulder injury while lifting weights and could no longer fully close his hand due to nerve damage. He then tried to play while wearing two blockers instead of a catching glove. Things didn't work out, and Blackburn retired when he was just 22 years old in 2005 after playing 63 career games.

4. Hall-of-Famer Johnny Bower debuted in the NHL with the Rangers as a 29-year-old rookie in 1953-54. He played all 70 games that season even though Gump Worsley won the Calder Trophy the previous season. Bower was sent back to the minors the next year, as Worsley won his job back, and would play just seven more contests with the Rangers. He was then taken by Toronto in the 1958 Intra-League Draft and went on to win four Stanley Cups and two Vezina Trophies.

5. The Rangers traded one Hall of Fame goalie for another in 1963 when Gump Worsley was sent to Montreal for Jacques Plante. Plante, who was the first goalie to wear a mask in an NHL game, had already won six Stanley Cups and Vezina Trophies when he arrived. He played 98 games over a season and a half with the Rangers before retiring in 1965. He then made a comeback in 1968 when St. Louis claimed Plante in the Intra-League Draft.

6. Harry Lumley may have played just one game for the Blueshirts, but he made history while doing so. Lumley was the property of the Detroit Red Wings but was loaned to the Rangers for a game in 1943-44. It was his NHL debut, and his name was written in the history books as being the youngest goalie to ever play in the league at 17 years of age. As of 2019-20, the record still stands.

7. Chuck Rayner debuted in the NHL with the New York Americans in 1940-41 but lost his job when the team folded in 1942 due to World War II. After three years in the Canadian Navy, he signed as a free agent with the Rangers

in 1945. He was then the team's starting goalie for six of the next seven seasons. Rayner won the Hart Trophy in 1949-50, and the three-time All-Star was inducted into the Hall of Fame even though he had a losing record.

8. The great Terry Sawchuk finished his career with the Rangers and sadly played just eight games in 1969-70 before he died. Sawchuk and teammate Ron Stewart were involved in a scuffle in the offseason with the goalie suffering internal injuries. He then died following two operations in a Manhattan hospital at the age of 40. Stewart was exonerated by a jury as Sawchuk's passing was ruled an accident. At the time of his death, Sawchuk was the NHL's all-time leader in wins at 447 and shutouts with 103.

9. Eddie Giacomin cemented himself as one of the best NHL goalies with the Rangers from 1965 to 1975. He led the league in shutouts and games played in four of his seasons and shared the Vezina Trophy in 1970-71 with Gilles Villemure. However, after missing the postseason for the first time in 10 years, Giacomin was claimed on waivers by Detroit in October 1975.

10. The last goalie to win the Stanley Cup with the Rangers was Mike Richter in 1993-94. He played his entire NHL career with the Blueshirts from 1989 to 2003. He became the first Rangers goalie to win 300 games, had his number retired by the club, and was inducted into the U.S. Hockey Hall of Fame. Richter still owns the club record for wins in a season, with 42, which he set in 1993-94.

CHAPTER 10:

ODDS & ENDS

QUIZ TIME!

1. This player was the first to captain two separate Stanley Cup-winning Rangers teams?

    a. Vic Hadfield
    b. Mark Messier
    c. Bill Cook
    d. Art Coulter

2. As of 2020, the Rangers have had how many general managers?

    a. 6
    b. 10
    c. 8
    d. 11

3. Pavel Bure was the last player to wear the number 9.

    a. True
    b. False

4. Which player scored the game-winning goal in the 1993-94 Conference Finals?

   a. Esa Tikkanen

   b. Mark Messier

   c. Stephane Matteau

   d. Glenn Anderson

5. How many hits did the team have combined in 2011-12?

   a. 2,047

   b. 1,792

   c. 1,338

   d. 2,419

6. How many years did the club's Stanley Cup drought last?

   a. 55

   b. 54

   c. 47

   d. 50

7. John Scott was one of the tallest players in the NHL. How tall is he?

   a. 6' 5"

   b. 6' 7"

   c. 6' 8"

   d. 6' 6"

8. Rod Gilbert was the first player in Rangers history to record 1,000 career points.

   a. True

   b. False

9. What technique did short-term Ranger Bernie Geoffrion popularize?

    a. Slapshot
    b. Wrist shot
    c. Drop pass
    d. Wrap-around

10. How many players blocked more than 100 shots in the 2018-19 season?

    a. 4
    b. 6
    c. 5
    d. 3

11. The team scored four hat tricks in their inaugural season.

    a. True
    b. False

12. Which goaltender allowed 13 goals and had two shutouts to win the club's second Stanley Cup?

    a. Dave Kerr
    b. Joe Miller
    c. Andy Aitkenhead
    d. John Ross Roach

13. How many seasons did Jaromir Jagr play for the Rangers?

    a. 2
    b. 4
    c. 5
    d. 3

14. Henrik Lundqvist won at least 30 games in each of his first eight seasons with the club.

    a. True
    b. False

15. How many hat tricks had the club scored by the end of the 2019-20 regular season?

    a. 275
    b. 267
    c. 280
    d. 301

16. How many seasons did the Rangers play in the Atlantic Division?

    a. 20
    b. 17
    c. 19
    d. 18

17. In 2008-09, John Tortorella replaced which Rangers coach?

    a. Alain Vigneault
    b. Bryan Trottier
    c. Tom Renney
    d. Glenn Sather

18. As of 2019-20, how many players (excluding goaltenders) have suited up and played at least one game with the Rangers?

    a. 1,000
    b. 983

c. 794

d. 971

19. How many wins did famous coach Fred Shero have while leading the club?

    a. 76

    b. 88

    c. 90

    d. 82

20. Of the teams from the "Original Six" era, the Rangers have won the fewest Stanley Cup championships

    a. True

    b. False

QUIZ ANSWERS

1. B – Mark Messier

2. D – 11

3. A – True

4. C – Stephane Matteau

5. D – 2,419

6. B – 54

7. C – 6′ 8″

8. A – True

9. A – Slapshot

10. D – 3

11. A – True

12. C – Andy Aitkenhead

13. B – 4

14. B – False

15. C – 280

16. C – 19

17. C – Tom Renney

18. B – 983

19. D – 82

20. A – True

DID YOU KNOW?

1. After the class of 2020 was announced, 62 former New York Rangers players and officials have made it to the Hockey Hall of Fame. This includes 54 enshrined as players and 8 in the builders category. In addition, 23 members of the franchise have received the Lester Patrick Trophy. This award was created in 1966 and is presented by the NHL and USA Hockey to honor those who have greatly contributed to ice hockey in the USA.

2. As of 2019, a total of 40 Rangers players had been named to the NHL's end-of-season First or Second All-Star Teams at least once. Lester Patrick was named the First Team coach seven times in the 1930s, including six in a row. In addition, 10 Rangers players had been named to the league's All-Rookie Team throughout history.

3. The Rangers went over half a century between Stanley Cups, as they won it in 1940 and not again until 1994. They beat the Vancouver Canucks in seven games in 1994 and were coached by Mike Keenan. The Rangers also won the Presidents' Trophy that campaign as the top team in the NHL regular season with a then franchise-record 112 points. That mark was beaten in 2014-15 when they earned 113 points.

4. The 1978 song "Double Vision" by the rock band Foreigner was reportedly inspired by Rangers goalie John

Davidson. The band were Rangers fans, and while watching a postseason contest between New York and Buffalo, Davidson was struck in the facemask by a shot. As the shook-up Davidson was recovering, television announcers Bill Chadwick and Jim Gordon remarked that Davidson was probably experiencing "double vision."

5. Former Rangers winger Michael Nylander currently has two sons playing in the NHL. William Nylander skates with the Toronto Maple Leafs, while fellow forward Alexander Nylander competes with the Chicago Blackhawks. Michael played 160 regular-season games as a Blueshirt from 2005 to 2007 and chipped in with an impressive 162 points in 160 outings with a +43 rating.

6. The Rangers' and New York Knicks' dressing rooms at Madison Square Garden are circular in shape. This is due to a suggestion by former Rangers captain and Hall-of-Famer Mark Messier in the 1990s as he believed it would be better for team unity. Messier believed a circular room would enable each player to look into their teammates' eyes.

7. There have been 35 different head coaches in Rangers franchise history, with Lester Patrick being the first in the inaugural 1926-27 season. The latest coach is David Quinn, who took over before the start of the 2018-19 season. Muzz Patrick and Emile Francis both had three stints as head coach, while Frank Boucher, Craig Patrick, and Phil Esposito had two.

8. There are several former head coaches who are enshrined in the Hockey Hall of Fame as players or builders. These are: Lester Patrick, Frank Boucher, Lynn Patrick, Neil Colville, Bill Cook, Doug Harvey, Emile Francis, Craig Patrick, Herb Brooks, Phil Esposito, Fred Shero, Roger Neilson, Bryan Trottier, and Glen Sather.

9. The most successful head coach in Rangers history was Lester Patrick as he guided the team to two Stanley Cups. He also coached the most regular-season games at 604 and playoff games at 65. The best winning percentage belongs to Mike Keenan at .667, and he led the team to the Presidents' Trophy and the Stanley Cup in 1993-94.

10. As far as general managers go, the Rangers have employed 11 in franchise history. These were Lester Patrick, Frank Boucher, Muzz Patrick, Emile Francis, John Ferguson Sr., Fred Shero, Craig Patrick, Phil Esposito, Neil Smith, Glen Sather, and current GM Jeff Gorton. Sather, Patrick, Shero, and Francis are in the Hall of Fame as builders, while Patrick, Esposito, and Boucher were inducted as players.

CHAPTER 11:

RANGERS ON THE BLUE LINE

QUIZ TIME!

1. How many points did the Rangers' blueliners combine for in their inaugural season?

    a. 9

    b. 14

    c. 28

    d. 30

2. Which defenseman has the most penalty minutes in franchise history, with 1,226?

    a. Ron Greschner

    b. Jeff Beukeboom

    c. Harry Howell

    d. Dave Maloney

3. Lester Patrick played three games on defense for the club in 1926-27.

    a. True

    b. False

4. Who was the first Rangers defender to score a hat trick?

    a. Yip Foster
    b. Sparky Vail
    c. Leo Bourgeault
    d. Bill Regan

5. How many points did Marc Staal post in the 2009-10 season?

    a. 18
    b. 29
    c. 15
    d. 27

6. Who was the only blueliner to block more than 100 shots in 2012-13?

    a. Dan Girardi
    b. Ryan McDonagh
    c. Anton Stralman
    d. Michael Del Zotto

7. Harry Howell played 21 years in the NHL; how many seasons were spent with the Rangers?

    a. 17
    b. 8
    c. 14
    d. 19

8. James Patrick led the team with 45 assists in 1986-87.

    a. True
    b. False

9. Doug Harvey scored how many game-winning goals in 1961-62?

    a. 5
    b. 1
    c. 3
    d. 2

10. Who has the most assists in a season for the club with 80?

    a. Sergei Zubov
    b. Harry Howell
    c. James Patrick
    d. Brian Leetch

11. Eleven defensemen suited up for the Rangers in the 1993-94 season.

    a. True
    b. False

12. How many goals did Anthony DeAngelo tally in 68 games in 2019-20?

    a. 12
    b. 15
    c. 19
    d. 24

13. Which defenseman had a plus/minus of -24 in 1976-77?

    a. Dave Maloney
    b. Mike McEwen
    c. Carol Vadnais
    d. Dave Farrish

14. Ott Heller was the only defenseman to play all 50 games in the 1943-44 season.

    a. True
    b. False

15. Which defender played 811 games, the ninth most with the team?

    a. Marc Staal
    b. Ron Greschner
    c. Dan Girardi
    d. Jim Neilson

16. Defender Marek Malik had a plus/minus of what in the 2006-07 season?

    a. +26
    b. -13
    c. +32
    d. -40

17. How many points did Brian Leetch, who led the team, get in the 1993-94 playoffs?

    a. 30
    b. 41
    c. 34
    d. 29

18. In his second season with the club, how many points did Sergei Zubov score?

    a. 89
    b. 77

c. 85

d. 79

19. How many penalty minutes did Ching Johnson have during his 11-year career with the club?

a. 745

b. 457

c. 268

d. 826

20. The most hat tricks in a Rangers season were scored by a defenseman.

a. True

b. False

QUIZ ANSWERS

1. C – 28

2. A – Ron Greschner

3. B – False

4. C – Leo Bourgeault

5. D – 27

6. A – Dan Girardi

7. A – 17

8. B – False

9. C – 3

10. D – Brian Leetch

11. A – True

12. B – 15

13. B – Mike McEwen

14. A – True

15. D – Jim Neilson

16. C – +32

17. C – 34

18. A – 89

19. D – 826

20. B – False

DID YOU KNOW?

1. There are 16 former Rangers blueliners in the Hockey Hall of Fame. These are: Bill Gadsby, Art Coulter, Doug Harvey, Tim Horton, Harry Howell, Ching Johnson, Brian Leetch, Brad Park, Earl Seibert, Allan Stanley, Sergei Zubov, Babe Siebert, Babe Pratt, Neil Colville, Lester Patrick, and Kevin Lowe. Colville, Pratt, and Babe Siebert all played defense and forward during their NHL careers.

2. The latest Rangers blueliner to be inducted into the Hockey Hall of Fame is Kevin Lowe as he was announced as part of the induction class for 2020. Lowe was traded to the Rangers in December 1992 from Edmonton, where he had already won five Stanley Cups. He then helped the Rangers hoist the Cup in 1993-94. Lowe then rejoined Edmonton as a free agent in 1996. He played 1,254 regular-season games in his career and another 214 in the playoffs.

3. Neil Colville joined the team in 1936 and helped the Rangers hoist the Stanley Cup in 1939-40. He centered the "Bread Line" with Alex Shibicky and his brother Mac but left in 1942 during World War II. Colville and his brother rejoined the Rangers in 1945 as blueliners and were the first brothers to play defense together in the NHL. After retiring, Colville became the Rangers' youngest coach in 1950-51. He captained the Rangers from 1945 to 1949 and was named an NHL All-Star as both a defender and forward.

4. Ivan Wilfred Johnson was known as "Ching" throughout his career and joined the Rangers in time for their inaugural season in 1926-27. He helped the squad win two Stanley Cups and was a four-time NHL All-Star. He earned the reputation as being one of the hardest hitters in hockey history, which made him a fan favorite. In 1937, Johnson disappointed those fans however by joining the rival New York Americans for his last NHL campaign.

5. Another hard-hitting defender to play for the Rangers was Tim Horton, who was acquired from Toronto in March 1970. He played a combined 112 regular-season and playoff games in New York before Pittsburgh claimed him in the 1971 Intra-League Draft. Buffalo then claimed Horton in the Intra-League Draft a year later. The 44-year-old lost his life in 1974 in a car accident following a game in Toronto. Horton, who played 24 years in the NHL, also founded the popular Tim Horton's fast-food restaurant chain.

6. When it comes to goals by a Rangers blueliner in one season, Reijo Ruotsalainen is the top dog with 28. He set the mark in 1984-85 when he also added 45 assists for 73 points. He notched 18 goals and 56 points as a rookie in 1981-82 and also scored 20 goals in 1983-84. Ruotsalainen scored 99 goals and 316 points in 389 regular-season games with New York and also played forward occasionally.

7. One of the most unheralded defenders in Rangers annals was James Patrick. He was drafted 9th overall by the team

in 1981 and would tally 467 points in 671 regular-season games with a +66 rating. He was traded to Hartford in November 1993 just months before the Rangers won the Stanley Cup. Patrick would go on to play 1,280 career games, score 639 points, and was a +100.

8. The second Ranger to win the James Norris Trophy as the NHL's top defender was Harry Howell in 1966-67 when he was also named to the First All-Star Team. The stay-at-home Howell played 17 years with New York and had his jersey retired in 2009. He played a team-record 1,160 games from 1952 to 1969 and notched 345 points. The Hall-of-Famer was then traded for cash to Oakland in 1969 and would play seven more years in the league before retiring.

9. Not really known for his physical play, blueliner Ron Greschner holds the Rangers' all-time record for penalty minutes at 1,226, with another 106 minutes in the postseason. Greschner played his entire 982-game career with the Rangers from 1974 to 1990 and chipped in with 610 points on 179 goals and 431 assists. He added 49 points in 84 playoff outings and was also used as a forward at times during his career.

10. Former captain Barry Beck was a physical presence on the blue line between 1979 and 1986 and also chipped in offensively. He scored 239 points in 415 regular-season games with a +75 rating and 775 penalty minutes. Injuries caught up to Beck, and he retired at the age of 30 in 1987. His rights were sold to Los Angeles in 1989, and Beck came back to play one final season with the Kings.

CHAPTER 12:

CENTERS OF ATTENTION

QUIZ TIME!

1. Mark Messier scored how many goals in the 1995-96 season?

   a. 50
   b. 47
   c. 18
   d. 36

2. Which center led the team with 37 goals in the 1982-83 season?

   a. Robbie Ftorek
   b. Mikko Leinonen
   c. Mike Rogers
   d. Mark Pavelich

3. Jean Ratelle had a plus/minus of -61 in 1971-72.

   a. True
   b. False

4. Which center scored six power-play goals in 2014-15?

   a. Derek Stepan
   b. J.T. Miller
   c. Derick Brassard
   d. Dominic Moore

5. How many hits did Brandon Dubinsky dish out in 2008-09?

   a. 251
   b. 207
   c. 265
   d. 189

6. Who was the only Rangers center to play all 82 games in 1999-2000?

   a. Manny Malhotra
   b. Petr Nedved
   c. Tim Taylor
   d. Mike York

7. How many centers played for the team in the 2018-19 season?

   a. 6
   b. 13
   c. 7
   d. 12

8. Scott Gomez played 196 games as a New York Ranger.

   a. True
   b. False

9. What is the most assists in a season by a Rangers center?

    a. 70
    b. 67
    c. 72
    d. 54

10. Which center notched 67 points in 62 games in 1975-76?

    a. Pete Stemkowski
    b. Wayne Dillon
    c. Walt Tkaczuk
    d. Phil Esposito

11. Wayne Gretzky scored only one regular-season hat trick with the Rangers.

    a. True
    b. False

12. Who won 682 faceoffs in 2011-12?

    a. Brad Richards
    b. Brian Boyle
    c. Derek Stepan
    d. Artem Anisimov

13. Which center tallied 48 goals and 33 assists in 1983-84?

    a. Chris Kontos
    b. Mark Pavelich
    c. Mike Rogers
    d. Pierre Larouche

14. The most penalty minutes Jean Ratelle ever had in a season was 28.

a. True

b. False

15. The club used how many centers in their inaugural season?

    a. 4
    b. 2
    c. 3
    d. 6

16. Who was the only center to score a shorthanded goal in 1989-90?

    a. Carey Wilson
    b. Mark Janssens
    c. Kelly Kisio
    d. Bernie Nicholls

17. Which center led the team in the 1996-97 playoffs with 20 points?

    a. Esa Tikkanen
    b. Wayne Gretzky
    c. Mark Messier
    d. Mike Eastwood

18. How many points did Pete Stemkowski score as a Ranger?

    a. 334
    b. 287
    c. 320
    d. 317

19. Which season was Petr Nedved's last as a Ranger?

   a. 1999-00
   b. 2001-02
   c. 2002-03
   d. 2003-04

20. Mark Messier's lowest point total with the Rangers was 23 in 2001-02.

   a. True
   b. False

QUIZ ANSWERS

1. B – 47

2. D – Mark Pavelich

3. B – False

4. C – Derick Brassard

5. A – 251

6. D – Mike York

7. D – 12

8. B – False

9. C – 72

10. D – Phil Esposito

11. A – True

12. A – Brad Richards

13. D – Pierre Larouche

14. A – True

15. B – 2

16. C – Kelly Kisio

17. B – Wayne Gretzky

18. D – 317

19. C – 2002-03

20. A – True

DID YOU KNOW?

1. There are 14 former Rangers centers in the Hall of Fame. These are: Mark Messier, Phil Esposito, Wayne Gretzky, Frank Boucher, Marcel Dionne, Pat LaFontaine, Edgar Laprade, Eric Lindros, Vaclav Nedomansky, Buddy O'Connor, Jean Ratelle, Howie Morenz, Max Bentley, and Clint Smith.

2. The greatest player in hockey history was arguably Wayne Gretzky, the NHL's all-time leader in goals, assists, and points. "The Great One" signed with the Rangers as a free agent in the summer of 1996 and announced his retirement three years later at the age of 38. In between, he played 234 games in New York with 57 goals and 249 points, with another 10 goals and 20 points in 15 playoff encounters.

3. Even though Hall of Fame center Marcel Dionne was 35 years old when he arrived in New York via a March 1987 trade with Los Angeles, he was still productive. Dionne racked up 98 points in 118 regular-season games before retiring in 1989. He was a four-time All-Star who won two Lester Pearson and Lady Byng Trophies in his career, as well as an Art Ross Trophy.

4. The Rangers nearly landed big center Eric Lindros in a deal with the Quebec Nordiques in 1991, and he eventually did end up in Manhattan in the summer of 2001. The Hall-of-Famer, who arrived in a trade with

Philadelphia, played 192 regular-season games with the team with 158 points to his name. He missed most of the 2003-04 season with injuries and signed as a free agent with Toronto in 2005.

5. Jean Ratelle was often compared to Montreal Canadiens' great center Jean Beliveau for his classy demeanor on and off the ice. Ratelle began his Rangers career in 1963, and it lasted until being traded to Boston in 1975. His career was nearly derailed before it got started as he underwent major spinal cord surgery when he was 23. Ratelle led the club in scoring from 1968 to 1973 and was the first Ranger to reach 100 points in a season.

6. One of the Rangers' early fan favorites was center Don Raleigh who played with the squad from 1947 to 1956 and captained the team from 1953 to 1955. However, he played 15 games for the team in 1942-43 when he was just 17 years old. He then spent three years in Canada before returning to the fold. Raleigh wasn't a big scorer but was a consistent one who notched 320 points in 535 games in Manhattan.

7. Frank Boucher helped the Rangers win Stanley Cups in 1927-28 and 1932-33. The Hall-of-Famer went on to coach the team to another Cup triumph in 1939-40 and later became the club's general manager. Boucher was a clean and slick player who won seven Lady Byng Trophies in eight years between 1927 and 1935. The trophy was then given to Boucher to keep while a replica was made.

8. Phil Esposito was another Rangers center who would play for, coach, and manage the team during his Hall of Fame career, after arriving in a blockbuster deal with Boston in 1975. It took Esposito a while to get rolling in New York, but in 1978-79, he led the team to the Stanley Cup Finals. He notched 20 points in 18 games that postseason as the Rangers were downed in five games by Montreal.

9. After the Second World War, center Edgar Laprade was signed by General Manager Frank Boucher and was named the NHL's rookie of the year for 1945-46. He notched eight points in 12 games during the 1950 playoffs when the Rangers lost the Stanley Cup Final to Detroit in double overtime of Game 7. Laprade won the Lady Byng Trophy for 1949-50 and notched 280 points in 500 games in his Hall of Fame career, which ended in 1955.

10. Bernie Nicholls was a high-scoring center who racked up 1,209 points in his 1,127-game career. He made a pit stop in Manhattan in January 1990 when he arrived in a trade with Los Angeles. He scored 110 points in 104 outings, with an impressive 11 goals and 19 points in 15 playoff contests. Nicholls was then traded in October 1991 in the deal that brought Mark Messier to New York from Edmonton.

CHAPTER 13:

THE WINGERS TAKE FLIGHT

QUIZ TIME!

1. Which winger scored 69 points in 2014-15?

   a. Kevin Hayes

   b. Martin St. Louis

   c. Mats Zuccarello

   d. Rick Nash

2. How many goals did Ulf Dahlen score in 1987-88?

   a. 29

   b. 32

   c. 25

   d. 38

3. In 2007-08, the club used 12 wingers.

   a. True

   b. False

4. Which left winger had 211 hits in 2014-15?

   a. Chris Kreider

   b. Tanner Glass

c. Jesper Fast

d. Chris Hagelin

5. How many points did Tony Leswick score in 1949-50?

a. 28

b. 37

c. 44

d. 50

6. Which winger scored the most goals in a season for the club?

a. Mike Gartner

b. Vic Hadfield

c. Adam Graves

d. Jaromir Jagr

7. How many power-play goals did Adam Graves tally in 1993-94?

a. 20

b. 15

c. 8

d. 26

8. Murray Murdoch was the first Rangers winger to score a hat trick.

a. True

b. False

9. Rod Gilbert is top point scorer in Rangers history; how many goals did he notch in his career?

a. 410

b. 398

c. 406

d. 375

10. Which winger has scored a franchise-high nine hat tricks?

a. Phil Esposito

b. Steve Vickers

c. Rod Gilbert

d. Bill Cook

11. Bill Cook played right wing on the famous "Bread Line."

a. True

b. False

12. This player had a plus/minus of +60 in 1971-72?

a. Bill Fairbairn

b. Vic Hadfield

c. Bruce MacGregor

d. Ted Irvine

13. In his first playoff appearance with the club in 2013-14, how many points did Martin St. Louis score?

a. 18

b. 10

c. 7

d. 15

14. Adam Graves is the only Rangers winger to crack the top 10 for most career penalty minutes.

a. True

b. False

15. How many games did Kevin Hayes play for New York in 2018-19 before being traded to Winnipeg?

    a. 35

    b. 44

    c. 51

    d. 62

16. Which winger earned 39 assists in 2001-02?

    a. Theoren Fleury

    b. Radek Dvorak

    c. Mike York

    d. Sandy McCarthy

17. How many goals per game did Lynn Patrick average in 1941-42?

    a. 0.68

    b. 0.64

    c. 0.71

    d. 0.66

18. Who led the team with 44 assists in 2009-10?

    a. P.A. Parenteau

    b. Ales Kotalik

    c. Marian Gaborik

    d. Ryan Callahan

19. How many consecutive seasons did Steve Vickers record at least 50 points?

a. 6

b. 3

c. 4

d. 7

20. In 1990-91, Mike Gartner led the team in shots taken with 270.

a. True

b. False

QUIZ ANSWERS

1. D – Rick Nash

2. A – 29

3. B – False

4. B – Tanner Glass

5. C – 44

6. D – Jaromir Jagr

7. A – 20

8. A – True

9. C – 406

10. D – Bill Cook

11. A – True

12. B – Vic Hadfield

13. D – 15

14. B – False

15. C – 51

16. A – Theoren Fleury

17. D – 0.66

18. C – Marian Gaborik

19. A – 6

20. B – False

DID YOU KNOW?

1. The 17 former Rangers wingers who made it into the Hockey Hall of Fame in Toronto, Canada, are the following: Glenn Anderson, Andy Bathgate, Doug Bentley, Pavel Bure, Bill Cook, Bun Cook, Dick Duff, Mike Gartner, Bernie Geoffrion, Rod Gilbert, Jari Kurri, Guy Lafleur, Lynn Patrick, Luc Robitaille, Brendan Shanahan, Bryan Hextall, and Martin St. Louis.

2. One of the first well-known American-born players in the NHL was right winger Cecil Dillon who played in the league between 1930 and 1942, and with the Blueshirts until 1939. He never missed a game with the team and led the squad in scoring for three seasons from 1936 to 1938. Dillon, who was a two-time All-Star, also helped the Rangers capture the 1933 Stanley Cup by scoring eight goals in the postseason to set a new record at the time.

3. Hall-of-Famer Bryan Hextall made his Rangers debut on right wing in 1936-37 and spent 11 years with the team. The four-time All-Star led the NHL in goals on two occasions and also led the league in total points with 56 in 1941-42, before the Art Ross Trophy was established. Hextall's biggest goal came in the 1940 Stanley Cup Finals against Toronto when he tallied in overtime to give the Rangers the Cup. His son Bryan Jr. and grandson Ron Hextall would later play in the NHL.

4. Adam Graves was never an NHL superstar, but he was a Rangers hero who had his jersey retired by the team. The power winger signed as a free agent from Edmonton in 1991 and set a new franchise record at the time with his 52 goals in 1993-94. He then scored 10 goals and 17 points in 23 playoff outings to help the Rangers hoist the Stanley Cup. Graves played 10 years with the Blueshirts and posted 308 goals in 840 combined regular and postseason games along with 880 penalty minutes. He also won the Bill Masterton Trophy for 2000-01.

5. Winger Vic Hadfield suffered numerous injuries as a Ranger but managed to become the first player in franchise history to score 50 goals in a season. He peaked in 1971-72 when playing on the "GAG Line" with Hall-of-Famers Rod Gilbert and Jean Ratelle. Hadfield scored 50 goals and 106 points that season and helped the Rangers reach the Stanley Cup Finals. He posted 572 points in 841 regular-season games with the team.

6. Because of his slippery ways on the ice, winger Camille Henry was nicknamed "The Eel." Henry was a power-play specialist who won the Calder Trophy for his outstanding 1953-54 rookie season in which he scored 24 goals, including 20 power-play markers. Henry then won the Lady Byng Trophy in 1957-58 and scored 256 goals and 478 points in 637 regular-season contests as a Ranger.

7. After playing just one game with the club in each of the previous two seasons, right winger Rod Gilbert broke in ⋯h the Rangers full time in 1962-63. He played his entire

120

career in Manhattan until 1977-78, won the Bill Masterton Trophy for 1975-76, and was a two-time All-Star. Gilbert accumulated 406 goals and 1,021 points in 1,065 games and still stands number one on the club's all-time scoring list. He added 67 points in the playoffs, including a team-record 34 goals.

8. Undrafted right winger Anders Hedberg was one of the first Swedish players to hit it big in North America when he played in the World Hockey Association (WHA) on a line with Bobby Hull and Ulf Nilsson in Winnipeg. Both Hedberg and Nilsson signed with the Rangers as free agents in 1978. Hedberg would score 397 points in 465 career games in New York until 1985, with a +53 rating. He added 22 goals and 46 points in 58 playoff encounters and took home the Bill Masterton Trophy for 1984-85.

9. Winger Andy Bathgate played the first 12 years of his Hall of Fame NHL career with the Rangers. He produced 272 goals and 729 points for the team in 719 regular-season contests and rarely missed a game. The four-time All-Star scored 40 goals in 1958-59 and won the Hart Trophy. He then tallied 28 goals and 84 points in 1961-62 to share the league lead in points with Bobby Hull. However, Hull was awarded the Art Ross Trophy as he scored more goals.

10. Martin St. Louis was never drafted into the NHL but would go on to post 1,033 points in 1,134 games and win a Stanley Cup. The 5-foot-8 Hall-of-Famer finished his career with the Rangers from 2014 to 2015 with 60 points in 93 regular-season games and 22 points in 44 playoff

outings. He led the team with eight goals and scored 15 points in the 2013-14 playoffs as the Rangers made it to the Stanley Cup Finals. St. Louis still holds the record for being the oldest player to lead the league in scoring at the age of 37 in 2012-13.

CHAPTER 14:

THE HEATED RIVALRIES

QUIZ TIME!

1. Which team had the Rangers lost 340 regular-season games to as of March 11, 2020?

    a. Detroit Red Wings

    b. Toronto Maple Leafs

    c. Montreal Canadiens

    d. Boston Bruins

2. Who did the Rangers NOT face in the 1993-94 playoffs?

    a. Vancouver Canucks

    b. New York Islanders

    c. Pittsburgh Penguins

    d. Washington Capitals

3. The rivalry between the Rangers and New Jersey Devils is known as the "Hudson River Rivalry."

    a. True

    b. False

4. In the 2014-15 regular season, how many teams did the Rangers NOT lose a game to?

   a. 5
   b. 9
   c. 2
   d. 10

5. Which New York Islanders defenseman was hated by the Rangers' fan base since 1979?

   a. Bob Lorimer
   b. Jean Potvin
   c. Stefan Persson
   d. Denis Potvin

6. How many goals did New York score against the Detroit Red wings in the 1985-86 regular season?

   a. 20
   b. 8
   c. 29
   d. 16

7. Which team did the Rangers play a 23-game series against on a European exhibition tour in 1959?

   a. Toronto Maple Leafs
   b. Chicago Blackhawks
   c. Detroit Red Wings
   d. Boston Bruins

8. The Rangers have won 1,095 of 2,019 games played at on Square Garden since 1969.

a. True

b. False

9. In the 1939-40 playoffs, the Rangers scored how many goals against Toronto?

   a. 12

   b. 8

   c. 14

   d. 18

10. The Rangers had a perfect record against which now-defunct franchise?

    a. Pittsburgh Pirates

    b. Montreal Maroons

    c. St. Louis Eagles

    d. Philadelphia Quakers

11. The Rangers went winless against 11 different teams in the 2003-04 regular season.

    a. True

    b. False

12. As of 2019, the Rangers had faced the Philadelphia Flyers how many times in the playoffs?

    a. 15

    b. 11

    c. 13

    d. 8

13. That was the score in a blowout win for the Rangers over Edmonton on October 24, 1979?

a. 10-0

b. 8-1

c. 12-0

d. 10-2

14. The Rangers and Philadelphia Flyers rivalry is referred to as "Broadway versus Broad Street."

a. True

b. False

15. The Rangers tied 103 games against which club?

a. Detroit Red Wings

b. Pittsburgh Penguins

c. New Jersey Devils

d. New York Islanders

16. Between 1975 and 1994, how many consecutive seasons did the New York Islanders defeat the Rangers in the playoffs?

a. 3

b. 6

c. 4

d. 7

17. What was the Rangers' record against the Ottawa Senators in 1926-27?

a. 1-2-1

b. 3-0-1

c. 2-1-1

d. 0-3-1

18. How many times have the Rangers eliminated the Washington Capitals from the playoffs?

    a. 7
    b. 5
    c. 3
    d. 2

19. As of 2019, how many times have the Rangers faced the New Jersey Devils in the postseason?

    a. 10
    b. 6
    c. 3
    d. 5

20. The club's rivalry between the New York Islanders is appropriately nicknamed the "Battle of New York."

    a. True
    b. False

QUIZ ANSWERS

1. C – Montreal Canadiens

2. C – Pittsburgh Penguins

3. A – True

4. B – 9

5. D – Denis Potvin

6. A – 20

7. D – Boston Bruins

8. B – False

9. C – 14

10. D – Philadelphia Quakers

11. A – True

12. B – 11

13. D – 10-2

14. A – True

15. A – Detroit Red Wings

16. C – 4

17. D – 0-3-1

18. B – 5

19. B – 6

20. A – True

DID YOU KNOW?

1. The Rangers have developed several rivalries due to being one of the NHL's "Original Six" franchises, as well as their close proximity to several other NHL teams. Their all-time playoff series records against the other Original Six squads as of 2019 were: Boston Bruins 3-7, Chicago Blackhawks 1-4, Detroit Red Wings 1-4, Montreal Canadiens 9-7, Toronto Maple Leafs 5-3.

2. The Blueshirts have met Montreal the most in the playoffs as they've battled 16 times and have been quite successful at 9-7 for a 56.3 winning percentage. However, they've lost both playoff series to Buffalo and the only one they've played against Tampa Bay. Meanwhile, they've played Calgary, St. Louis, Colorado, Winnipeg, Vancouver, and Florida once each in the postseason and won every series.

3. At the end of the 2018-19 postseason, the Rangers had been involved in 108 playoff series with a record of 53-55 against 21 different clubs. They had winning records in series against 11 of those franchises, with losing records against nine of them and an even record against one club. In addition, the Rangers are just 4-7 in Stanley Cup Finals.

4. The "Hudson River Rivalry" between the Rangers and New Jersey got its name since they're cross-river enemies. They've met six times in the playoffs, with the Rangers winning four series and two of those going the full seven

games. The most famous meeting came in 1993-94. New York had gone 6-0 against the Devils in the regular season but had to fight back from a 3-2 series deficit in the Conference Finals. Three of the games went to double overtime, including Game 7. The Rangers then went on to win the Stanley Cup.

5. The "The Battle of New York" is between the Rangers and New York Islanders, with the Blueshirts winning just three of the eight playoff meetings. They've fared better in the regular season though with a 130-116-19-9 mark at the end of 2019-20. The Islanders were a powerhouse in the late 1970s and through the 1980s and dominated the Rangers, but things have turned around since the Blueshirts' Stanley Cup-winning season in 1993-94.

6. The Rangers have developed a rivalry with fellow Metropolitan Division team the Washington Capitals since 1979. The teams met three times in the playoffs in a five-year span in the 1990s and five times in a seven-year stretch between 2009 and 2015, with four of the series going a full seven games. The Rangers hold the edge 5-4 in playoff series wins but have lost more individual playoff games as well as regular-season contests. Combined, the Capitals hold an all-time lead at 138-118-8-8.

7. The intense Rangers vs. Philadelphia rivalry is known as "Broadway vs. Broad Street." The Flyers hold a 6-5 lead in postseason series wins, with three of them going the distance. Six of these playoff meetings came between 1980 and 1987. They played a legendary series in 1974 when the

Rangers became the first Original Six team to lose a series to an expansion team. It went seven games with Philly's Dave Schultz severely pounding Dale Rolfe in the decider with no Rangers stepping in to help.

8. The cities of Boston and New York don't get along in any sports, and hockey is no exception. The Rangers and Bruins have met 10 times in the payoffs, with New York winning just three series. They also lost in the Stanley Cup Finals to Boston in 1929 and 1972. In regular-season and playoff games combined, the Rangers' record against Boston is 278-322-99 for a 46.9 winning percentage.

9. One of the most infamous incidents in the Rangers vs. Bruins rivalry occurred during a regular-season game at Madison Square Garden on December 23, 1979. The incident followed Boston's 4-3 win when several Bruins players climbed over the glass to fight with fans. Boston's Mike Milbury then attacked a supporter with his own shoe after ripping it off the fan's foot. Three players were suspended following the melee, lawsuits were filed, and higher glass was installed in the rink.

10. Another bizarre incident took place at Madison Square Garden in a 1971 playoff game against Toronto. With five minutes left in the game, Toronto's Jim Harrison fought with Vic Hadfield. Leafs goalie Bernie Parent jumped in, and Hadfield ripped off the netminder's mask and threw it into the crowd. Parent wouldn't play without it, so Jacques Plante entered the game. Just 34 seconds later, a bench-clearing brawl ensued with both goalies included. This

resulted in 160 penalty minutes with four players being ejected. Parent's mask showed up 41 years later after it was sold at an auction.

CHAPTER 15:

THE AWARDS SECTION

QUIZ TIME!

1. As of 2019, how many Rangers rookies have won the Calder Memorial Trophy?

    a. 10

    b. 8

    c. 4

    d. 6

2. Who was the first member of the franchise inducted into the Hall of Fame as a builder?

    a. William M. Jennings

    b. Emile Francis

    c. John Kilpatrick

    d. Lester Patrick

3. Chuck Rayner was the first goaltender in the club to attend the All-Star Game.

    a. True

    b. False

4. How many members of the club have received the Lester Patrick Trophy as of 2019?

   a. 25
   b. 19
   c. 23
   d. 14

5. Which player won the first major NHL award for the team in 1927-28?

   a. Clarence Abel
   b. Lorne Chabot
   c. Bill Cook
   d. Frank Boucher

6. How many games did Henrik Lundqvist win when he was awarded the Vezina Trophy in 2011-12?

   a. 40
   b. 39
   c. 38
   d. 37

7. What was Michael Rozsival's plus/minus when he won the NHL Plus/Minus Award in 2005-06?

   a. +34
   b. +55
   c. +35
   d. +41

8. Despite playing three seasons with the Rangers, Wayne Gretzky's number 99 is not retired by the franchise.

a. True

b. False

9. As of 2019, how many Rangers have won the Ted Lindsay Award?

    a. 3
    b. 5
    c. 4
    d. 2

10. Which team trophy has been won only three times as of 2019?

    a. Stanley Cup
    b. O'Brien Trophy
    c. Prince of Wales Trophy
    d. Presidents' Trophy

11. Mark Messier is the only Ranger to have won the Conn Smythe Trophy as of 2019.

    a. True
    b. False

12. Adam Graves did NOT win which of the following awards?

    a. NHL Foundation Player Award
    b. Bill Masterton Memorial Trophy
    c. Ted Lindsay Award
    d. King Clancy Memorial Trophy

13. How many times has the club won the Prince of Wales Trophy as of 2019?

a. 4

b. 5

c. 3

d. 2

14. John Vanbiesbrouck was the first Rangers goaltender to win the Vezina Trophy.

a. True

b. False

15. How many points did the team have when they won their first Presidents' Trophy?

a. 97

b. 105

c. 112

d. 109

16. Which Ranger won the Lady Byng Trophy seven times?

a. Lester Patrick

b. Frank Boucher

c. Mike Gartner

d. Rod Gilbert

17. Wayne Gretzky captured the Lady Byng Memorial Trophy in which season?

a. 1995-96

b. 1996-97

c. 1997-98

d. 1998-99

18. How many Rangers were named to the end-of-season All-Stars Teams for 1971-72?

    a. 1
    b. 8
    c. 4
    d. 6

19. Which was the first major trophy awarded to a member of the club?

    a. Vezina Trophy
    b. Lady Byng Memorial Trophy
    c. Hart Memorial Trophy
    d. Calder Memorial Trophy

20. As of 2019, no member of the Rangers franchise has won the Art Ross Trophy, Jack Adams Award, or Frank J. Selke Trophy.

    a. True
    b. False

QUIZ ANSWERS

1. B – 8

2. C – John Kilpatrick

3. A – True

4. C – 23

5. D – Frank Boucher

6. B – 39

7. C – +35

8. B – False

9. A – 3

10. D – Presidents' Trophy

11. B – False

12. C – Ted Lindsay Award

13. A – 4

14. B – False

15. B – 105

16. B – Frank Boucher

17. D – 1998-99

18. D – 6

19. B – Lady Byng Memorial Trophy

20. A – True

DID YOU KNOW?

1. The Rangers franchise has won numerous individual and team awards since 1926-27. These include: Stanley Cup (4), Prince of Wales Trophy (4), Presidents' Trophy (3), Bill Masterton Memorial Trophy (5), Calder Memorial Trophy (8), Conn Smythe Trophy (1), Lester Patrick Trophy (21), James Norris Memorial Trophy (4), Lady Byng Memorial Trophy (15), Hart Memorial Trophy (4), Ted Lindsay Award (3), and Vezina Trophy (4).

2. Since the following trophies were introduced, no Ranger has ever won the Art Ross Trophy for leading the league in point-scoring, the Rocket Richard Trophy for leading in goals, the Frank J. Selke Trophy as the top defensive forward, and the William M. Jennings Trophy for allowing the fewest goals against. In addition, no Rangers coach has won the Jack Adams award as coach of the season.

3. Eight New York players have won the Calder Trophy as the NHL's top rookie. Kilby MacDonald was the first in 1939-40 followed by Grant Warwick in 1941-42, Edgar Laprade in 1945-46, Pentti Lund for 1948-49, goaltender Gump Worsley in 1952-53, Camille Henry in 1953-54, Steve Vickers in 1972-73, and Brian Leetch in 1988-89.

4. The Conn Smythe Trophy for the MVP of the playoffs has been won by just one Rangers player. Defenseman Brian Leetch was honored for his work in the 1993-94 postseason

when he tallied 11 goals and 23 assists for 34 points in 23 games to help the team capture the Stanley Cup.

5. Three Rangers blueliners have combined to win the James Norris Trophy on four occasions as the NHL's best defenseman. Doug Harvey took the honors for 1961-62, with Harry Howell winning it for 1966-67. Brian Leetch then took it home for his play in 1991-92 and 1996-97.

6. Many Rangers have been rewarded for their sportsmanship, ability, and gentlemanly conduct with the Lady Byng Trophy. Frank Boucher won it seven times in eight years with awards from 1927-28 to 1930-31 and from 1932-33 to 1934-35. Clint Smith won it for 1938-39 and was followed by Buddy O'Connor in 1947-48, Edgar Laprade in 1949-50, Andy Hebenton in 1956-57, Camille Henry in 1957-58, Jean Ratelle in 1971-72 and again in 1975-76, and Wayne Gretzky in 1998-99.

7. From 1927 to 1981, the Vezina Trophy was for the team allowing the fewest regular-season goals. New York's winners were Dave Kerr in 1939-40, while Eddie Giacomin and Gilles Villemure shared it in 1970-71. In 1982, the Vezina was then handed to the NHL's top goalie with the William M. Jennings Award for the fewest goals conceded. John Vanbiesbrouck won the Vezina for 1985-86, while Henrik Lundqvist won it again in 2011-12.

8. The Hart Memorial trophy is awarded to the player deemed most valuable to his team during the regular season. Blueshirts players to take this honor have been

Buddy O'Connor in 1947-48, Chuck Rayner in 1949-50, Andy Bathgate in 1958-59, and Mark Messier in 1991-92.

9. The Ted Lindsay Award is given to the player who was chosen as the most valuable in the regular season by his peers in the NHL Players' Association. Jean Ratelle won it for the Rangers in 1971-72, while Mark Messier took it home in 1991-92, and Jaromir Jagr followed suit in 2005-06.

10. Perseverance, sportsmanship, and dedication to hockey is rewarded each year with the Bill Masterton Trophy. Rangers who have received this honor have been Jean Ratelle in 1970-71, Rod Gilbert for 1975-76, Anders Hedberg in 1984-85, Adam Graves in 2000-01, and Dominic Moore for 2013-14.

CONCLUSION

The book you've just read through contains almost 100 years' worth of trivia, facts, and anecdotes regarding the famous New York Rangers NHL franchise, starting with their NHL debut in the 1926-27 season.

We trust that you've been entertained with the information provided and hope some of the team's best moments triggered some fine memories for you. If you've been able to learn something new along the way, then even better.

The Rangers may have endured a Stanley Cup drought of over half a century, but the team has still provided its fans with plenty of thrills, action, and drama—even during the lean times.

We've tried to present the information in a lighthearted and fun manner when it comes to describing the players, coaches, management, and officials. We have tried to vary the trivia and facts as much as possible, but realize there's still quite a bit of Rangers' history that isn't included.

The most loyal Rangers fans may know most of the answers to the questions included, and probably have a few stories of their own to tell. With the knowledge these fans possess, and the information included in the book, they'll be in the perfect position to challenge fellow Blueshirts supporters when it comes to quiz time. They may even be able to convert a few neutral fans or those of rival NHL teams over to the Rangers while they're at it.

The Rangers may not be the most successful NHL franchise in history, or even in America for that fact, but they are one of the most storied and revered. Those who fill the seats in the hallowed hall known as Madison Square Garden to cheer them on realize they could witness NHL history in the making on any given night.

With fans like that, it's no wonder Rangers home games are among the most exciting and unpredictable in the world of sport. Thanks for being one of those fans and for taking the time to read through the Rangers trivia book.

Made in United States
North Haven, CT
10 December 2022

28438263R00083